I0841028

Empath Made Easy

How to Thrive in a Chaotic World by Utilizing Your Unique Ability, Developing Your Gift and Mastering Your Personality Using Simple Psychological Tactics for Everyday Use

Michael Wilkinson

Copyright © 2018 Michael Wilkinson

All rights reserved.

No part of this publication may be reproduced, stored in a retrieval system, or transmitted, in any form or by any means, electronic, mechanical, photocopying, recording, or otherwise, without the prior written permission of the author and the publishers.

The distribution, uploading, and scanning of this book via the Internet, or via any other means, without the permission of the author is illegal and punishable by law.

Please ensure only authorized electronic editions are purchased, and do not engage in or promote electronic piracy of copyrighted materials.

Disclaimer

This book is not aimed at offering any medical advice or representing medical treatment or advice from your personal healthcare provider. Readers should consult their personal physicians or licensed health professionals concerning their medical conditions and treatments. The author shall not be held responsible or liable for any misuse or misinterpretation of the information provided in this book. The information is not intended for diagnosis, cure or treatment of any ailment.

Be reminded that the author of this book is not a medical professional/doctor/therapist. Only opinions on the basis of personal experiences and research are referenced. The author does not provide any medical advice or prescription of any treatments. Consult your doctor for any medical or health issues.

It is important to note that I research all of the material in my books to bring you the highest quality material. Unfortunately, there are substandard, cheap outsourced books on the non-fiction market nowadays which are developed by different Internet marketing organizations. My aim is to ensure you are provided with only high quality contents as **I do not compromise the high quality of my books**.

Table of Contents

Introduction
Chapter 1: What it Means to be an Empath

Common Traits
Types of Empaths

Chapter 2: Empath Quizzes for the Unsure
Chapter 3: How to Embrace Your Gift

It's Not a Curse
Balancing Emotions
Prevent Emotional Drainage

Chapter 4: Simple Coping Mechanisms for Any Situation
Chapter 5: Even Science Understands Empaths

Emotional Contagion
Electromagnetic Fields
Increased Sensitivity of Dopamine
Synesthesia
Psychologies View

Chapter 6: Understanding Energy Effects

Humans and Vibrational Energy
Sensitivity to Energy

Chapter 7: A Societal View on Empaths
Chapter 8: How to Protect Yourself from Energy Vampires

Identifying Energy Vampires
Protect Yourself

Chapter 9: Problems that Empathy can Cause
Chapter 10: How to Handle Empathy in Your Life

Relationship Sabotage
Empathy at Work

Chapter 11: Become More Self-Aware
Chapter 12: Normalizing, Fine Tuning and Maintaining Your Gift

Controlling Emotions

Chapter 13: Keeping Out Unwanted Emotions
Chapter 14: Healing

Important Truths
Clearing Emotions

Chapter 15: How to Support a Young Empath
Chapter 16: Exercises You Can do Daily
Conclusion

Also, if you haven't downloaded your free book already:

<u>The Growth Mindset: How To Become The Best Version of Yourself</u>

To help speed up your personal transformation, I have prepared a special gift for you!

<u>Download my full 88-page e-book "The Growth Mindset: How To Become The Best Version of Yourself"</u>

Visit this Link:

https://www.developsucccssmindset.com/mindset-gift/

Introduction

I want to congratulate you on taking all those so important first steps on your journey to self-awareness and love so that you can use your gift to help others and yourself. If you have chosen to purchase this book, I am guessing that you have just realized that you could have the gift of empathy. There are likely a lot of emotions swirling through your mind right now and you could be a little scared. Being scared is normal because you probably don't understand what empathy is. Excitement may also be prevalent because you are ready to take this journey and learn about this new world and everything that it can bring you.

For the most part, empaths who haven't learned how to control their abilities will likely experience a lot of anxiety, nervousness, and maybe even physical pain. When you start feeling the emotions of others so much so that they feel like your own emotions, you can wind up on a rollercoaster of feelings that you can't understand. This book is here to help you come to a place of peace with your ability. You are going to learn exactly what it means to be an empath and why it makes you such a special person.

It's important that you understand you have a lot of power in you. The reason why it has such a deep effect on you is that of how dynamic it is. Being an empath will bring you many gifts and benefits. As you begin to embrace all that you can do, you will notice that opportunities will open up to you that you didn't know were there.

Make sure that you completely absorb and take in every chapter in this book before you continue on. You need to make sure that your spirit is ready for what you are going to learn and unlock with the information found throughout these pages. You will be amazed at the potential that you have living within you.

Chapter 1: What it Means to be an Empath

A simple definition of empathy is having an ability to understand and read people and resonate or to be in tune with others. This can be either voluntary or involuntary. If you are a natural empath, the latter will be true for you.

Empaths are hypersensitive and experience high levels of understanding, compassion, and consideration to others. Their extreme empathy creates something of a tuning fork effect, where they can feel the emotions of the people that they are around. Many empaths are normally unaware of how this works. They have probably accepted the fact that they just feel more sensitive toward certain people.

It doesn't matter whether or not they know it, empaths share many of the same traits that other empaths have.

Being an empath means that you get affected by other people's energy and you have the ability to intuitively feel and perceive others who are around you. Unconsciously, you get influenced by other people's wishes, moods, thoughts, and desires. Being an empath is a lot more than just being super sensitive and it isn't limited to just emotions.

Empaths can perceive spiritual urges and physical sensitivities. They can understand the intentions and motivations of others. A person is either an empath or they aren't. It isn't anything that you can learn. You are open to process other people's energy and feelings. This means you can actually feel, and in many cases, take on the emotions of others. Many empaths will experience things such as unexplained aches and pains, chronic fatigue, or environmental sensitivities each day. All of these can be attributed to outside influences and not so much about yourself. You are basically walking around with a whole lot of accumulated energy, emotions, and karma that has come from others.

Empaths are quiet achievers. They don't like getting compliments because they like to point out other people's achievements. They are very expressive in various areas of emotional connections and they can talk openly and sometimes very frankly. They don't have any problems talking about their feelings as long as someone will listen to them.

They could, however, be the total opposite — reclusive and unresponsive at the best of times. They might sometimes appear to be ignorant. Some have even gotten good at blocking people out and this isn't a bad thing, at least for an empath who is learning and struggling with a huge amount of emotions from others and their own feelings.

Empaths are usually open to feeling what is outside of them more than what they are feeling inside. This means that empaths have a tendency to ignore their own needs. Empaths are usually non-violent, non-aggressive, and most of them are peacemakers. Areas that have a lot of disharmonies can cause empaths to feel very uncomfortable. When they are in the center of a confrontation, empaths will try to settle the situation as quickly as they can, if they don't avoid it completely. If they say something harsh when defending their self, they usually resent their lack of self-control.

Empaths can pick up on other's feelings and project them back without even knowing where they came from. Talking things out is very important for an empath who is learning so they can release emotions. Empaths might develop stronger degrees of knowledge so they can find peace in any given situation.

Empaths can also be very sensitive to videos, movies, news, broadcasts, and television. Violent or emotional dramas that show shocking scenes of pain that were inflicted on children, animals, or adults might bring them to tears.

Empaths might find they like working with people, animals, or nature. They are passionate to help others when they can. They are usually tireless caretakers and teachers for our environment and everything that lives in it.

They can be amazing storytellers because of their ever-expanding knowledge, endless imagination, and inquisitive minds. They are extremely gentle and old romantics at heart. They are usually the "keepers of family history and ancestral knowledge." If they aren't obvious family historians, they are usually the ones who listen to stories that have been passed down and they possess most of the family's history.

They might have a broad interest in music that suits all of their temperaments. The people who are closest to them might question how they can listen to a certain type of music and then a few minutes later, they have changed to something completely different. Song lyrics could have powerful effects on empaths, especially if it is relevant to things they are or have experienced.

Common Traits

While every empath is a little different, they do share some common traits that can be easily spotted.

1. Many are introverted

Crowds usually overwhelm them as it amplifies their empathy. They like to have one-on-one contact with people or little groups. Even if they are a bit more extroverted, they still try to limit the amount of time they spend at parties or in crowds.

2. Highly Sensitive

Empaths are great listeners. They give naturally. They are open spiritually. If you need someone with heart, you need to find an empath. These nurturers will help you no matter what. Their feelings can be easily hurt. Most empaths have been told they need to "toughen up" or are just "too sensitive."

3. Highly Intuitive

Empaths experience the world through their intuition. This is a skill they have to develop so they can learn how to listen to their gut feelings about others. This helps them stay away from negative people and find relationships that are positive.

4. They absorb emotions

They are very in tune with the moods of others, whether they be good or bad. They sometimes feel everything at extremes. They will consume negative emotions. This causes them to become exhausted. When surrounded with love, their bodies will flourish.

5. Intimate relationships can become overwhelming

Being together a lot can be hard on empaths and they might steer away from being intimate with others. Deep down, they are afraid of losing their identity. For an empath to feel at ease in their relationship, their normal paradigm needs to be redefined.

6. Nature replenishes empaths

Everyday life can be hard on an empath. Nature can help nourish and restore them. It helps them release their burdens. They take refuge in the presence of bodies of water especially the ocean and green things in nature.

7. Alone time

Because of their heightened senses, empaths find it to be draining when they are around a lot of people. They need to have some alone time in order to recharge themselves. Just a short escape will keep them from having an emotional overload. One good example is that empaths will often choose to drive themselves places so that they will be able to leave whenever.

8. Energy vampire targets

Their sensitivity can make them an easy mark for energy vampires. These people will do more damage than just damaging their physical energy. Narcissists are very dangerous and could make their victim feel as if they are unlovable.

9. Tuned senses

Empaths might find their nerves are easily frazzled by excessive talking noise or smells.

10. They just know

Empaths know things without being told. This is a knowing that is more than intuition or gut feelings. They might describe their understanding in this way.

11. Sometimes gives too much

Empaths have big hearts and they will try to help other people's pain. It is natural for them to reach out to those who are in need and try to ease their suffering. Unfortunately, empaths don't stop with just that. Instead, they consume their problems and feel upset and completely drained.

12. Addictive personality

Empaths will sometimes turn to drugs, sex, alcohol, or other addictions in order to block out emotions. This is their form of self-protection to help them hide from others and things.

13. Easily distracted

School, work, and their home life need to be interesting otherwise they will switch off and just start to daydream or doodle.

14. Drawn to metaphysical and holistic things

Even though many empaths love to heal others, they will turn away from being a healer even after they have been qualified because they will take on too many emotions from their patients. This will happen more if they don't actually know they are an empath. Empaths are open to things that others consider unthinkable. They don't get surprised or shocked easily.

15. Low back problems and digestive disorders

The solar plexus chakra is in the middle of the stomach and is the seat of emotions. This is where empaths will feel other people's emotions and this causes this area to weaken. This can lead to anything from stomach ulcers to IBS. Low back problems could happen if they are ungrounded, along with other problems. A person who doesn't know they are an empath will always be ungrounded.

16. They can read honesty

If they have a loved one or friend lying to them, they will know it instantly. Many empaths will try not to focus on this fact because they get hurt knowing a person close to them is lying to them.

Types of Empaths

Many people don't realize there are different types of empaths. If you're an empath, it is important that you know which one you are so you can make the most of your gift and can take care of yourself.

1.   Physical or Medical Empath

These empaths can pick up on the bodily energy of the people they are with. They can instantly tell what is bothering another person. Many people who have this type of empathy will be a healer either in the alternative or conventional sense. They might feel awareness in the body when they treat someone else. They might notice blockages in someone's energy that should be treated.

A medical empath will notice symptoms in others and might feel these same symptoms in their own body. Once they take on the physical symptoms of others, this could lead to other health problems. People who have chronic illnesses such as fibromyalgia or an autoimmune disease might find it to be helpful to strengthen their energy field so they can turn off their abilities when they need to. If you can train yourself in a specific type of healing, it might help you strengthen this ability.

2. Emotional Empath

This is the most common type of empath. These empaths will pick up people's emotions easily when they are around others and they take on the emotions like they were their own. They experience other people's feelings deeply in their own body. For example, emotional empaths can become extremely sad around people who are experiencing sadness.

It's important for an emotional empath to be able to tell the difference between their emotions and the emotions of the people they are near. Once they can do this, they can help people without completely draining themselves.

3. Plant Empath

These empaths can intuitively know what a plant needs. They have a green thumb and are gifted for putting the right plants in the right places in their homes or garden. Many will work in wild landscapes, gardens, or parks where they can use their gift for the greater good. In fact, if you are in an occupation that involves plants, there is a good chance that you are a plant empath. Many people will receive guidance from plants or trees by hearing what is in their mind.

If you are a plant empath, you know that you need a lot of contact with trees and plants. You could strengthen this bond by sitting quietly near a special tree or plant and tuning into it to see if it needs anything.

4. Geomantic Empath

This type of empathy is often referred to as environmental or place empathy. These empaths are closely connected to the physical landscape. If you feel uncomfortable or very happy in various situations or environments, you might be a geomantic empath.

These empaths will feel deep connections to various places. They might be pulled to groves, churches, sacred stones, or other areas with lots of power. They might also be able to pick up the history of places and might feel the sadness, joy, or fear that could have happened in that area many years ago. They are very connected with the natural world and hurt deeply when it gets damaged.

This empath needs to spend a lot of time in nature. They might also find it healing to help on any projects that help the environment. It is important to create beautiful and harmonious surroundings for your everyday life. They will feel happier if their house is full of natural plants and smells.

5. Claircognizant or Intuitive Empath

This empath will get information from others just by being near them. Just a glance will give them all sorts of insights. They will know if other people are lying just because they can sense these intentions. People who have this gift will resonate with other people's energetic fields and will be able to read their energy.

People who have this ability should surround themselves with people who they are aligned with. They might have to strengthen their own energetic field. This will ensure that they don't get bombarded with thoughts and emotions of others.

6. Animal Empath

The majority of empaths will experience a connection to animals, but an animal empath might devote their entire life to caring for our furry little friends. People who have this particular gift understand the needs of an animal and some might even be able to communicate with them.

If this is your empathy type, you are probably surrounded by animals already. The study of the psychology or biology of animals may help you to improve your talents. You might even consider becoming an animal healer because your talent might help you to figure out what ails them.

Chapter 2: Empath Quizzes for the Unsure

You might be wondering if there is a way to know for certain if you are an empath or not. It is more up to you to understand yourself and figure out if you are one or not. There is a test to help you determine if you are an empath or not.

Chances are if you have ever felt another person's pain or felt the energy in a room change without understanding what happened, you are probably an empath. We're going to see how much of the following you can connect with.

For every statement, give it a "3" for always, "2" for sometimes, and "0" for never.

1. You begin to feel drained when you are near certain people.

2. You can sense when others are in pain or sad.

3. You experience intense negative or positive impressions when you first meet a person and it ends up being correct.

4. You immediately know when somebody says one thing but means something else.

5. Most people don't understand how deeply you feel and why you can't let things go.

6. When you witness something sad such as an animal being abused, it takes you a long time to stop feeling upset about it.

7. You sometimes feel like you can feel the entire world's pain.

8. You can't watch sad or violent movies or read the news because it upsets you too much or it makes you feel sick.

9. You feel as if you look at life from a perspective different than everyone else. It feels almost like you're the only one.

10. You have days where you become so overwhelmed by the pain in the world that you would rather just hide out at home than face anybody.

11. You feel sick or in pain when you are around specific people for no physical reason or you feel as if you take on another people's symptoms and feelings.

12. You constantly feel the exact same sensations when you are near certain people. Each time you are with a specific friend, you might feel mad for no reason

13. You walk into a place and feel different energy without understanding the reason for it. For example, you walk into your office and get hit with sensations of frustration.

14. You feel like your mood changes when specific people come into a room.

15. You feel like your mood changes quickly but you don't know why.

16. You get overwhelmed when there are many people around but you don't understand why you are feeling overwhelmed.

17. People get pulled to you and want a "fix" to make them happy. You may even find that children and pets are pulled towards you.

18. People look at you as their "energy source" since you can brighten their day or you help their emotions.

19. Walking through nature is the only thing that makes you feel good.

20. You like being near water, especially when you feel overwhelmed.

21. You have a tendency to care about those around you instead of caring about yourself and you feel as if you must help everyone else, even if you are feeling burned out.

22. People ask you why you are "a bleeding heart" or they make fun of you because you feel things very deeply.

23. You have times in your life where you went through traumatic times and you felt completely numb.

24. You understand that animals and plants have awareness or souls and you can feel their emotions.

25. You have a hard time taking care of yourself since you always take care of others.

Now take a few minutes to add up your scores.

If you scored between zero and 25:

You do have some traits of an empath, but you aren't considered to be one. It is important that you make sure you are taken care of and be sure not to get overwhelmed. There is a chance you already have a decent balance between setting boundaries and helping others.

If you scored between 25 and 50:

You're an empath. You can feel things a bit differently than a normal person. You don't just relate to a person's feelings, you feel them like they're yours. You might feel exhausted a lot and don't understand why, since you don't know, you give out too much energy and you take in a lot of negativity. You may be balanced. There isn't any doubt that you are going to benefit from different resources that will help you with the new found power.

If you scored between 50 and 75:

If you are in this range, you are known as an extreme empath. You soak in others' emotions without knowing you are doing so. You can feel the energy of the room without having any visual cues. With a score this high, you are very open to suffering and pain in the world. You will get too overwhelmed by doing too much. If you don't work on your traits, you might wind up getting very sick.

Chapter 3: How to Embrace Your Gift

Once you have come to the realization that you are in fact an empath, it will be like somebody has removed a blindfold. All of a sudden things will make sense. Your feelings, interactions, experiences, and thoughts with others will be understood and seen against your personality type.

Labels have been thrown at you your entire life. You were likely called troubled, sensitive, or weak. Now you have discovered a label that fits perfectly. This is going to be the best feeling in the world. You have found a new identity, a sense of self, and a belief that you can explore your inner and outer workings with more confidence and knowledge.

After you understand that you're an empath, you won't feel alone. You will get to join a unified collection of others that share your gift. You will be filled with knowing you belong. This is likely something that you haven't gotten to experience in some time. You start to scour the internet trying to find places that empaths go such as forums, blogs, support groups, and Facebook. You will feel thrilled once you find them. There aren't just a couple of options either. You will find literally thousands of empaths.

Once you have come to understand that you are an empath, the words you know will expand. You will start talking about vibrations, lightworker, shielding, intuitive empath, grounding, and much more. This will all become normal for you.

You will begin to learn more about what empaths can do for the world, what challenges they have to face, and opportunities that come to them due to their abilities. While you work to research your new skills, you will shed some light on things that have happened to you in your past. Feeling a good or bad vibe when you meet a person without speaking to them, you now understand. You will now understand why you don't like getting bad news or being stuck in crowded places.

After you know that you are an empath, you will understand why everybody likes to come to you with all of their problems. You have always been the perfect listener and everybody is able to tell that, even if they don't know why.

For your entire life, you have been the person that your friends came to when they needed a shoulder to cry on. Up until now, it has probably felt like a burden, but now you understand. You start to realize that you have the talent of being able to see through another's eyes, walking in their shoes, and feeling how they feel. This means that you have taken in their sadness and despair while you were helping them to work through their feelings. You now have a good understanding of why this happened.

Once you have realized you are an empath, you will be able to learn how to handle your abilities. Just the ability to identify as one will allow you to find help for problems that you have been going through. The tool chest you have that was empty is now filling up as you become more confident about embracing the world around you.

You no longer have to be shy and fearful of the feelings of people, sensations, and places. You will likely not feel completely relaxed when you're outside of your comfort zone, but you will be willing to head outside of your comfort zone from time to time.

Once you know you are an empath, you will start to recognize that this is who you are and you are always going to be like this. You will learn how to change and grow with time, but the truth is that you are always going to be an empath. This can be a little bit disheartening and a lot liberating.

You now understand your essence and you will be able to quit trying to figure out ways to silence your natural tendencies. You will accept yourself and show those around your true self.

You will also have to deal with the struggles you will have to face. This is never going to stop. You will become better at coping but there are going to be times when your mind is going to cause feelings of sorrow and sadness.

Once you know you're an empath, you will notice your world has changed forever. You will have more explanations for things and you will understand more of who you are. You will be able to enter into a new chapter in your life. You will be reborn into a new you, one where you no longer feel lost. You will discover your true self. You will be able to celebrate your wholeness.

It's Not a Curse

You are likely very sick of hearing people tell you that your sensitivities make you weak. Those sensitivities are exactly what allow you to experience life at different depths. Sensitivity is what allows you to listen to your needs and dreams. Sensitivity allows you to help those around you. Sensitivity will let see the divinity of life and its beauty.

An untrained empath will likely be in constant pain due to their abilities. Your emotions will be a constant roller coaster and you will likely stay confused. This doesn't have to be the case.

Once you have learned how to surrender, observe, accept, and release, it will turn into just another aspect of you. The word soar in a simple definition means "to fly or transcend." This means that you will be able to learn how to soar over all the emotional darkness and congestion while you live your life as you.

Let's take a look at how you can SOAR:

- Surrender – first you have to learn how to relax your whole body. Take a deep breath in. Surrender any tension or discomfort that you may feel. Make sure you don't fight this. Feel all of the emotions that you are holding in. Before you surrender them, make sure you identify what the feelings are.

- Observe – allow yourself to feel your emotions. Do not judge them. How do they sound, smell, look like, and taste? Make sure you use all of your sense to create an image of them. The anxiety inside could feel like slime that squishes to your core. If all of your energy is clashing, it could feel as if you have a raging fire inside of you. Remember that you need to observe these and don't allow them to attack you. This is going to be a lot easier said than done. Allow the feelings to rise up and flow, just like an ocean tide.

- Accept – as you observe the emotions and sensations that are in you, accept them. Do not resist them. Welcome them in as a temporary visitor. They are going to leave. Nothing is going to remain forever.

- Release – as you are going through the motions of the past steps, you will start to feel these emotions slip away. Extremely intense and repressed emotions could end up rearing their ugly heads. Don't let these worry you. Carefully go through all of the steps as often as you have to so that you can get rid of them

You should practice this technique like a meditation. Set aside a few minutes every day to relax and calm yourself. There are lots of different ways that you can do this such as listening to calming music, walking barefooted outside, humming, focusing on your breath, and visualizing.

You are basically learning how to self-soothe. Figure out a practice that will work for you. If you aren't able to center yourself, you won't be able to succeed with the practice that is coming up.

To help you out, here is a sample grounding process:

You may notice that you are feeling anxious or sick. A lot of people are around you that could be sending out bad vibes, are demanding, laughing, gossiping, or just being loud. You must take a break. You are getting ready to take a break. This is the time for you to center and focus.

You are taking your lunch break. You start to feel tired and you are filled with an angry and impatient energy. If you can, sit outside on the Earth. Take in a few deep breaths. Notice the ground under you. Feel how the wind touches your face. You can center yourself in nature more easily.

Sit very still and breathe for a full ten minutes. If you have to, set a timer. You have started to feel grounded but you are still holding in restlessness. It tastes bad and appears to you like a storm cloud. Watch it. Let it be there. It could manifest in your stomach, shoulders, or neck. Let it be and watch. You remain grounded in nature. Watch and accept. It is there, so don't fight it.

Let a few more minutes pass. Shift your focus to how you feel and consciously experience your emotions. Be present with the uncomfortable sensations. Notice how it starts to slip away. Notice as it leaves your body and meets your consciousness. Watch it fade away.

Bring yourself back to the present and understand that your negative feeling has gone.

You will have to experiment with the procedure. You must make it work for you. This procedure is here to help you create mindfulness without experiencing attachment or resistance. You mustn't be rigid when you follow this. Allow it to naturally flow. If you meet an emotion with acceptance and no attachment, it is going to slip away.

Empaths tend to suffer because they are unconsciously attacked by things around them.

Balancing Emotions

Being an empath can be challenging but it can also provide benefits to you and those around you. In order

for you to experience the benefits, you will have to understand how to make it work so that you don't become a victim to the emotions of other people. Here's how:

- You are first

This tends to go against everything that has been ingrained in your brain. When you make sure that your needs have been met, you will be able to take care of those around you better. Empathy works best when you aren't depleted.

You must make sure that you are taken care of all the time. If you aren't, you are going to find that you are filled with the needs of others. Figure out things that will allow you to be a better you:

- o Meditate

- o Become a pen pal

- o Learn yoga

- o Get lots of sleep

- o Take an art class

- o Make dinner for a loved one

- o Exercise

- Set up boundaries

You can only function with so many thoughts and feelings in your head and heart. You need to limit what you take in from others. You have to accept the fact that you are only human and you can't help everybody.

If a person needs to talk with you about something in their life, set a time limit. This isn't because of a lack of love. This is so that you can support them the best way you can. If you allow yourself to be exhausted physically or emotionally, you are going to shut down and your empathy will lack.

Be conscious of all the information that you consume. The world is full of lots of happiness. But there is also a lot of sadness and injustice. Do your best to avoid an emotional rollercoaster. Limit the time you spend on social media or watching the news. As an empath, you can get caught up in the stories of others and you will forget to take care of your emotions. This can happen even if you don't know the person all that well.

- Release everything

It's amazing when we are able to celebrate with others. As an empath, you will feel what others feel. You will experience the joys of a child, wedding, and promotion. You also feel hopeless when you hear about somebody else's loses like losing a loved one, being diagnosed with cancer, or a rough breakup.

This is where separation can help. The fact of the matter is you didn't break up with anybody, you aren't fighting a disease, and nobody in your family has passed away. When your friends are around, you show them acceptance by letting them know that you love them. It's important that you understand that you don't have to embrace or keep their situation.

Feel it and let it go. Figure out how you can release a person's emotions. Find a person who can help you release these emotions. Since they aren't close to the situation, they won't hold onto it and they will help you. You have to deal with your own hurt. You don't have to help everybody else as well.

- Process emotions

The majority of empaths can sympathize with other people but they will neglect their needs. They become numb to their needs from all of the emotions they feel from others. This has to stop so that you can process your emotions.

Nobody has to be an island. Just because those around you bring in their feelings and thoughts doesn't mean you must rely only on yourself. Everybody needs some sort of guide to help them. Emotions can be handled formally or informally. The important thing is that you practice it regularly. Try:

- o Go to lunch with your best friend once a week.

- o Keep a journal.

  - o Process your emotions with somebody before bed.

  - o Talk to a spiritual leader.

  - o Go to a trained therapist.

  - o Find a life coach.

  - o Go to group counseling.

- Celebrate

As an empath, you know how to experience pain and joy. You will notice that pain is what likes to stick to you and will weigh you down. When you feel these negative emotions, it's important that you learn how to be emotionally balanced. Carrying the pain of others isn't helpful.

Celebration is a great way to bring positive rhythms into your life. It doesn't matter what is going on in your life, you can always celebrate. Try a few of these:

  - o Throw a party because you dropped a pound.

  - o Spend time with your kids.

  - o Take yourself on a date.

  - o Take a co-worker to dinner to celebrate their promotion.

  - o Give your partner a gift just because.

Empathy is a great way to allow others to know they feel connected and understood. Don't let yourself get exhausted. You need a balanced life so that you don't experience resentment. Let it empower others, but put yourself first.

Prevent Emotional Drainage

It can be overwhelming to have other's emotions constantly bombarding you. Empaths bring light and love along with their compassion. Experiencing the emotions of others comes with downsides. All of the negativity can deplete you. Other people will sometimes take advantage of you. To make sure that you thrive, it's important that your energy is protected. This is the only way that you can make sure that you can take care of others.

The following six ways can up your powers without being depleted by other's emotions:

1. Alone time

It's important for empaths to find alone time to get away from the negativity, drama, and stress of the world. If you don't take time alone, you will likely start feeling overwhelmed. You should make it a priority to find some alone time and use this time to whatever it takes to stay balanced and healthy. Writing in a journal, taking a walk outside, or meditation can help you to work through your own emotions.

2. Create an energy space

This is a space that will restore you. You should try to find a calm and peaceful space where you can't be distracted by the outside world. Some people will create a space in nature or in an empty space in their house. You could even lock yourself in your bathroom if you have to. Your space should be beautiful and full of candles, places, or artwork. Find stuff that puts you in a state of calm. That space should not be cluttered or untidy. The cleanliness will put your mind at ease. Essential oil or incense can help to improve the calmness.

3. Protection from negativity

You have to make sure that you protect yourself from negativity when you can. Limit the time that you spend with negative, toxic, and critical people. You need to find the time to restore when you have been around them. Avoid negative media and focus on positive things. Fill your world with inspiring things and quit allowing yourself to be pulled into other's negativity. Visualizing a ball of gold light wrapping itself around you when you notice you are being pulled into negativity is a great practice. This allows negativity to bounce off of you instead of you absorbing it.

4. Remove negative energy

It doesn't matter how great you are at protecting yourself, you will pick up bad emotions. You could find yourself stuck in bad thinking patterns. Empaths aren't able to be upbeat and positive all the time. The grief of the world will often bring you down into depression. You don't have to think of these emotions as negative. Grief and sadness are perfectly normal. If you deny this, it isn't going to go away. You need to feel these emotions completely and allow them to disappear. You should dance, exercise, and journal to help process the negativity.

5. Help the world with your ability

Empaths understand that problems won't be solved with hate or rejections. Instead, you have to solve them with love and understanding. Make use of your energy in a positive way to help others. It could be small things like cleaning up litter or donating some time at a food bank. Doing something good will help you to remain positive about being an empath instead of feeling as if it is a burden.

6. Chase your dreams

Empaths will often neglect their dreams because they remain sensitive to the needs of others. You need to remember that you are a unique human being. You were placed on earth for a reason. Don't allow other people to take all of your energy so that you don't have enough to follow your dreams.

Make sure that you take the time to follow your desires and make them something sacred. If you don't make a conscious effort and decision on how you are going to spend your energy, others are going to spend it on what they want. You will end up missing your purpose.

Empathy is a true gift. Being sensitive needs to be managed in order to make sure that you have the energy to live. Take some time to support you. This isn't selfish, it's necessary. This is the only way you can successfully share your gift with the world.

Chapter 4: Simple Coping Mechanisms for Any Situation

There are a lot of techniques in this book that can help you stay balanced and grounded, but sometimes you need something that you can access quickly. The following coping mechanisms can help you out when you are faced with a tough or stressful situation.

1. Water

The body is 75% water and a lot of body tissue is 95% water, so it shouldn't be a surprise that water is the top at the self-healing list. A lot of people aren't aware of the fact that they are dehydrated. Not enough water will create issues with how your physical and energetic bodies function. It also affects your general wellbeing and advances the aging process.

Water is a great protector for empaths and it's important that they have a lot of it inside and outside of their body. Most should aim for eight glasses of water each day to replenish what you naturally excrete through sweating, urination, and so on. The heavier you are, the more you should drink.

Water can also wash away things. Washing in water is not only good for your hygiene. Water is also able to cleanse your energetic body and remove negativity. When you find yourself in an emotional situation, grab a glass of water.

2. Create a shield

There are going to be situations that you rather avoid, but you can't because of the significance in your life. Important work functions, family get-togethers, and social events could involve energies that you find hard to deal with.

You will have to find a way to cope with these circumstances. To do this, you can create a mental barrier that will allow you to control what comes through and deflect the negativity. Imagine that you have a golden bubble surrounding you. Here you can focus inwards and find a balance with the troubles on the outside. When your energy starts to drain, you have the bubble to retreat inside of to stop the flow.

3. Repeat affirmations

Empaths tend to be open and giving people but this doesn't mean they are always positive. To remain positive even in negative situations, it's a good idea to have some positive affirmations that you can repeat to yourself to push away the negativity. Try this one the next time you are feeling down: "When I am with draining people, I will protect my own energy. I will create good boundaries. I will tell people 'no' when it is right. I will strengthen my relationships that serve a positive purpose."

4. Switch up your views

As an empath, it can be frustrating to interact with others. You have a higher ability when it comes to being kind and caring for people and when you notice others being harmed in any way, it hurts.

Because of this, it's a good idea to get out of your mind and watch the other person not as evil or bad, but as hurting or misguided. Most of the time, people who act opposite to you, do so because of how they were brought up or some form of trauma. They probably have a hard time envisioning the world the way you see it, so they don't act as you do.

When you change your perspective, you will reduce how they hurt you. You might even find some sympathy and love for them instead of frustration and bewilderment.

Chapter 5: Even Science Understands Empaths

Many things in life might appear to be magic until we can figure out how they work and understand the process involved. Unfortunately, the discovery for empaths is still being done. There has been a research done on mirror neurons and it is placing some light on the possible explanation for why empaths can experience other people's emotions.

Mirror neurons are thought to be a neurophysiological mechanism involved in how we understand other people's actions and learn to imitate them. There were first studies in the context of motor skills and they found that they fired up when a monkey watched another person perform a certain action. This brought them to a hypothesis that watching someone will trigger an internal response to help us imitate and mimic what we see. The act of watching another person experience something activates the neurons in our brain even when we don't actually perform this action. (Acharya & Shukla, 2012)

Marco Iacoboni introduced that mirror neuron might have the potential physiological basis for empathy and morality since they are involved in the way we perceive and interpret the experiences of those around us. In their simplest form, these neurons are triggered through observation of a physical gesture in another person that fires the same neurons in the person observing. What is amazing about this is that it happens consistently even though the person observing isn't moving anything. It works only on an internal representation of the actions and not a physical limitation.

For example, at a baseball game, neurons that get activated by the catcher when he catches the ball are also fired in the audience. This same process is also working when we watch somebody experience some form of physical pain or if we notice a certain facial expression of anger or worry. Our brain can interpret the meaning of these situations by experiencing them internally through its own mirror neurons. There are many ways to trigger mirror neurons — seeing a ball gets kicked, hearing the sound the ball makes when it gets kicked, or say the word kick could cause your mirror neurons to get fired up.

The firing pattern of mirror neurons is very sophisticated. In fact, the pattern is dependent on the meaning or context of the action that is observed like raising your hand to grab a ball or raising your hand if you have a question. Both actions involve the same muscles but they don't have the same intentions, so they trigger different mirror neuron pathways.

This is why Iacoboni believed that the firing patterns of these neurons are complex enough that it will let people know the intent of another person depending on the action's context. The presence of the process is important when you begin to think about how relating and understanding other people are important in our ability to survive in society. This gets supported by different bodies of research on the process known as emotional contagion. (Iacoboni, 2009)

Emotional Contagion

This is a process where a group or a single person influences the behavior of other people or groups through either an unconscious or conscious induction of behavioral attitudes and emotional states. This is a process that has deep roots in the human psyche. Studies show that newborns will imitate the facial expressions of other people within a few minutes of being born.

Even adults tend to imitate other people's demeanor, often unconsciously. This mimicry causes emotions from one to another and plays a big role in our social relationships. In fact, people are more likely to like a person that imitates them. It is thought that mimicry can make us feel more connected to others. It also gives us a positive emotional experience. This emotional contagion comes from basic mimicry as we work to feel loved by those who are around us. From birth, we spontaneously register and try to reproduce non-verbal language.

Even though science has ventured quite far, the empath experience seems to indicate that there is a human process where humans can innately sense other people's emotions in ways that aren't completely controlled by their conscious mind. Empaths wouldn't mind being able to turn off this every now and then so they can feel their own emotions. However, this experience is unconscious and uncontrollable. Most empaths have reported feeling overwhelmed by other's emotions without wanting to experience them. (Barsade, 2002)

Typically, when someone wants to improve a skill they make a conscious decision to do so and this gets followed by some sort of practice program and learning experience. There are some who are better at this than others so their need to practice might be shorter. For empaths, the physical manifestation happens first. They begin to feel what other people feel and they don't even realize what is going on. It is only after this has happened that they begin to embark on their quest to understand what is happening. Many empaths first thought is "How do I stop this?"

Being an empath never presents itself as a learned skill. It isn't something that a child can wish to have and then develop with practice. The initial trigger is usually a physiological one that leads to an emotional experience and then to conscious awareness. They will feel first then understand their gift later. Most say they don't have any control over the process. This means empathy is an innate ability and not everyone will experience this. Very little of the population will have this ability. Everyone can perceive a person's emotions. Only empaths have the unusual sensitivity to feel emotional cues.

Electromagnetic Fields

This finding is based on the fact that the heart and brain generate an electromagnetic field. According to HeartMath Institute, these fields send information about a person's emotions and thoughts. Empaths are particularly sensitive to this input and are usually overwhelmed by it. They have stronger emotional and physical responses to changes within the electromagnetic fields of the sun and earth. Empaths understand that everything that happens to the sun and earth will have an impact on their energy and state of mind. (McCraty, Atkinson, Tomasino, & Tiller, 1998)

Increased Sensitivity of Dopamine

Dopamine is a neurotransmitter that increases the activity of neurons and is connected to the pleasure response. Research shows that introverted empaths are typically more sensitive to dopamine than extroverts. This means they require less dopamine to be happy. This might explain why they are more content with meditation, reading, and alone time. They don't need external stimulation from social gatherings. Extroverts need a dopamine rush from those types of events. They can't seem to get enough of it.

Synesthesia

Synesthesia is a neurological condition where two senses are paired in the brain. For example, a person can see when they hear a specific piece of music or they taste words. Some famous synesthetics include Billy Joel, violinist Itzhak Perlman, and Isaac Newton. However, when it comes to mirror-touch synesthesia, people can feel the sensations and emotions of others in their body as if it were their own pain.

Psychologies View

Psychology has used the term empathy for a long time to describe a person's ability to see what other people might be feeling. This is also known as "walking in someone else's shoes." Empathy plays an important part in our social interactions. Empathy can affect how we act toward other people. It works like a glue that holds humans together.

Theodore Lipps has always been considered to be the father of the term empathy. He described it as how we perceived the mental state of those around us through a process of inner imitation. The process involves different areas in the brain like the endocrine system, hypothalamic-pituitary-adrenal axis, autonomic nervous system, and the cortex.

Even though people who have some psychopathologies like sociopaths can exhibit a lack of empathy, this skill has a strong biological foundation. Babies can recognize different types of emotions at a very young age and toddlers can develop empathy as they grow. Young children can identify the emotions of other people as well as interpret them correctly.

Recent studies have described two different systems that are involved in psychological empathy — an emotion-based contagion and a cognitive perspective-taking system. Emotional empathy seems to activate what is known as the inferior frontal gyrus. Cognitive empathy is more tied to the motor mirror neuron system. Rogers' model of empaths is closer to cognitive empathy than emotional empathy. (Riess, 2017)

Psychological experiments that study empathy will often use observation in order to trigger a person's empathic response. They will have the empath watch someone who is placed in a situation that is supposed to elicit strong emotions.

Rogers says that empathy involves an "as if" condition. A person could experience empathy when they can imagine what another person feels. This isn't any different than what empaths experience. Empaths feel things as their very own. It isn't something that is imagined or coming from external stimuli.

Chapter 6: Understanding Energy Effects

Energy or Universal Energy is the very basis of human existence. The electricity that gives power to your home, the gas that fuels your car, the sun that warms your body, are all forms of that energy.

Universal energy sustains all life and brings important energy to all things that live. The entire Universe, beginning with the stars to the little atoms that make them, as well as the world and human bodies, everything that we do or say is full of Universal energy at its core.

While we might see the world and everything that is in it as something physical or material, Quantum Physics thinks that everything exists was created by this energy that continuously flows and can change forms. Even Nobel Prize-winning scientists have proven this fact. Since we are normally viewing ourselves and the tangible things that are around us, it is hard to accept things as just energy.

These scientists have found that our "reality" is made up of atoms. There are millions of small vortexes of energy that vibrates and spins. They look like teeny, tiny tornadoes. Whether we see things as a solid, gas, or liquid all depends on the speed that the atoms move at.

Humans and Vibrational Energy

Since energy gives everything a vibration that decides its nature and the things it created, all humans have a vibration. The physical phenomenon of vibration and the spiritual vibration that we have inside us are different things.

The best capacity and power that man has is being able to receive and express thoughts. These thoughts are a combined form of this universal energy directed and created by a certain entity.

When trying to explain a thought, it's important to explain that the person who came up with it must be in control, but very few people are successful at doing just that. A thought, therefore, is a compact form of energetic manifestation. (Brown, et al., 2014)

The energy that vibrates on the low end of the spectrum moves slowly and tends to be dense and tangible. The human form tends to have slow wavelengths, in the scheme of the universe. Since we are a lower frequency, we view our selves as tangible and physical beings.

People feel that they are separate from everything and everyone because their energy vibrates at different frequencies from the things that exist around them. However, we are intrinsically connected to everything around us because our energy communicates, absorbs, interlocks, connects, and interacts with the other energy.

Sensitivity to Energy

There are those who are more in tune with the vibrations of the universal. They typically feel the environment's energy and even the energy of people that they aren't related to.

As the planet's vibration grows, more and more people are becoming receptive to this Universal energy surrounding all of us. The following signs will let you know if you are more sensitive to the world's energy.

1. You can feel the cycles of the moon

Every month of the year, the moon cycles from New to Full. The moon phases represent different emotions. Sensitive souls have a tendency to be extremely synchronized with these lunar phases.

While full, empaths will often feel a desire to end something in their life. There are some empaths who will find it hard to understand the power that the moon has over them. This will sometimes cause them to feel off during specific times.

2. Feel uncomfortable in crowded areas

Empaths will feel very overwhelmed and angry when in crowded spaces or public places. The reason for this is due to the fact that they can feel the energy of those who are around them.

Sensitive people and empaths have a tendency to notice their environment more and this includes certain smells, lights, and sounds that could end up becoming overwhelming. This becomes too difficult for them to fix, which is why they need to learn how to protect themselves.

3. Their intuition is on point

Empaths are extremely conscious of their environment, the energy of those around them, and this makes their intuition strong. They will end up knowing things before it happens or they are able to feel when a close friend is going through a rough patch.

4. They seek spiritual connections

Those who have more sensitivity to energy will have deeper desires to connect with somebody on a spiritual level, create a spiritual family, or a home that they are able to deeply resonate with.

5. Extreme dreams

Empaths tend to have vivid and intense dreams that are creative, which they will remember in great detail. For these people, dreaming becomes a chance to experience places and dimensions and explore different levels of reality.

6. Spiritual development

Because they are so creative, empaths yearn to learn about what their soul needs. Empaths are willingly open to every moment so that they can view the world from different perspectives. They will usually experience a spiritual awakening through things like opening their third eye and accessing their Kundalini energy.

7. They want to find purpose

For empaths, their life isn't just about simple pleasures, material security, family, or work. They feel like their life is deeper and bigger. They will spend much of their time trying to find their real purpose

Empaths want to be a positive impact on the world and they will try to make a personal contribution. Since that will often become their focus, they may end up feeling disappointed by people who don't share their same viewpoint.

Chapter 7: A Societal View on Empaths

When talking about living as an empath, there are two ways that things could go. Society will either support you, is interested in your gifts, and love you for it, OR they think there is something seriously wrong with you, you are too sensitive, or melodramatic.

It is great when society is supportive, but how many times have you ever been called these things: melodramatic, temperamental, weak, fragile, wussy, feeble, wimpy, thin-skinned, spineless, or overly sensitive. This is something that most empaths have to face.

Empaths can happen in an estimated five percent of the population. The ability that empaths possess is both a blessing and a curse. They can become amazing listeners and counselors. They know how to comfort people and they will assist the people around them. They find these jobs painful and tiring and it is worse when people don't understand them or just write them off as "weird."

Most of society will tend to be more open to empaths now than in the past. More empaths are cherished for their wonderful gift. They are still faced with a lot of misguided perceptions. Let's look at some of these societal myths and debunk them.

1. Empaths are psychologically frail.

The truth is, they are biologically programmed to be sensitive and to be in tune with their environment.

Empaths walk around with the entire world's accumulated problems and this can cause inner emotional tension for them. This is why they are more prone to showing signs of "weakness" and crying.

Empaths also find it hard to take part in normal activities. They feel emotions more deeply than others, which mean they are viewed as "weak minded", "wussy", or "frail."

2. Empaths are self-absorbed and navel-gazing.

Empaths focus more on others than themselves. Empaths are unexplainably moody and quiet on the outside at times. The reason for this has nothing to do with them being self-absorbed. Instead, they are deeply affected by the exterior emotions of those around them that they feel like their own.

3. Empaths are lazy.

Truth is, they lack physical, emotional, and mental energy because of their intense empathic abilities to understand other people.

Empaths have been diagnosed with headaches, insomnia, fibromyalgia, and chronic fatigue syndrome. When their body is continuously overloaded with stress, pressure, and tension, it gets translated into their body. This will often result in some form of illness. When they lack energy, they will often prefer to relax instead, but this in no way makes them lazy.

4. Empaths are mentally ill.

The truth is, they are magnets of negative energy. This will cause them to have a psychological imbalance.

Empaths are great listeners, counselors, and confidants. Because of this, people are drawn to their caring natures just like a magnet. This means that empaths are going to experience a lot of emotional dumping from others. They will sometimes have a hard time releasing all that negative energy.

Unfortunately, this will cause them to have lingering depressive feelings. This means empaths might appear to be mentally ill, and for some, this might be true. However, to the majority, they are just congested with the remnants of harmful emotional energy.

Chapter 8: How to Protect Yourself from Energy Vampires

By now you should have a fairly good understanding of what an empath is. Let's look at some new terms. When I say vampire, I'm not talking about the bloodsucking kind, although, they do suck in their own way.

First, there is a psychic vampire. This is used to describe the type of person who drains another person emotionally either empathically, meaning drying up their auric life force, or metaphorically, meaning somebody who takes emotionally but doesn't reciprocate. Psychic vampires are the type of people that were born with either an active or latent need, a physical need for life energy which they aren't able to supply themselves. They are people who have a psychological dependency on this pranic energy.

Then you have an energy vampire. This is the type of person who feeds off the energy or life force of other living creatures, mainly other people. They are sometimes also referred to as emotional vampires, energy parasites, psy-vamp, energy predator, empathic vampire, or pranic vampire.

Emotional vampirism refers to the act of manipulating another person into a desired intense emotional position like anger, passion, or love so that they can absorb the emotional energy. This vampirism includes practices like learning what a person needs in a partner and accentuating those types of traits in order to trick the person into thinking that they love them.

Now that we have covered some definitions, we can begin to look at how to stay away from these situations and be able to pick out those energy vampires.

I would like to get my PSA out of the way first. I want all empaths to know that it is okay to get rid of any relationships with a person you find out to be an energy vampire. There isn't any way to change them and it will continuously be a parasitic relationship. You will give them everything you have just to make them happy and they will just suck the life force right out of you. You will constantly feel drained, fatigued, and all around crappy. They get everything in the relationship.

Alright, back to what an energy vampire does. These people are known to make threats, manipulate people, are notorious guilt-trippers, flip out at random times, are deceptive, pick fights, cause unnecessary problems, and feed off of negative attention.

While energy vampires isn't a clinical term or diagnosis, Christiane Northrup, MD, explains that many energy vampires tend to map into "cluster B" personality disorders. These are people who tend to have erratic behavior or thinking, are overly emotional, or overly dramatic. Cluster B includes people who have narcissistic, borderline, and antisocial personality disorders. These are people whose disorders aren't caused by a chemical imbalance in the brain. Instead, they are individuals who have a somewhat misguided or a lack of a conscience or moral compass. According to Northrup, energy vampires are often those at the extreme end of this spectrum of personality disorders, mainly sociopaths and psychopaths.

For the most part, psychic vampires aren't ill-intentioned or evil. In their minds, they are victims. They think they are helpless, paranoid, powerless, strive for perfection that can never be reached, engage in extremes, self-medicate, and are preoccupied with always being right.

These people don't realize that they can create their own reality. They lack mentality. They always focus on the things that they don't have. They don't think it is possible to attain the love they desire. They don't think that they can fulfill their own needs. This means that they believe the only way to get their needs fulfilled is by taking them from others.

Empaths and highly sensitive people are more susceptible to these types of people because the emotional vampire is drawn to your warmth, bright energy, and compassion. The emotional vampire will feast on those qualities to satiate their needs until you are feeling sick and completely drained.

Empaths can be drawn to these people because they think they are in need. The thing is, energy vampires don't want to be healed. They aren't looking for somebody to save them. All they want is the attention you give them when all they have is an unnecessary and self-created problem that they crave.

These people are survivalists. As long as they are able to find a food source — you, they don't have any need to be healed or take care of themselves. The more you try to fix them, the more problems they have that start popping up.

Here are some facts. Around 20 percent of all people, female and male, have characteristics of an emotional vampire or they are full-blown vampires. That comes out to one in five people. And every one of them affects five people. That's almost 60 million people indirectly or directly affected by these people. That means that it is very likely that you are in a relationship with or know a person who is an emotional vampire.

The energy vampire could be a person you think of as a friend, a colleague, or even a parent. Chances are, though, unless you've been threatened by them, you probably don't realize that you are dealing with one because they are extremely charming, until they decided to come after you.

All of a sudden you are blindsided by insults, being shamed for all different things like how you talk, your income level, where you come from, body size, age, or social status, and you can even be abused. Energy vampires often become distant and moody, which causes you to walk on eggshells. This only causes you to expend more energy while admiring and praising them to try and keep the peace. This impacts your self-esteem so much that you believe something is really wrong with you.

When you live with this constant stress and low self-esteem caused by this person, it could lead to chronic inflammation because of your high levels of cortisol. This can cause you to indulge in other behaviors like alcohol, drugs, or bad dietary choices. This only causes more cellular inflammation and can end up leading to disease. In fact, a lot of empaths won't realize they are dealing with an energy vampire until they have become physically ill.

What really sucks is the fact that you could open your door to these people through your own insecurities. You yourself could feel powerless or feel like a victim. You could be an approval seeker. Co-dependence problems are their golden ticket.

There is a chance that you only feel good with yourself when you are helping others. You could even feel unworthy of friendships or love unless you do something. You could also feel guilty for experiencing good fortune when so many other people seem down on their luck.

You might even be addicted to energy vampires. Do you enjoy feeling needed? Do you need to please people? When you are around an energy vampire, do you feel better about yourself?

You might even be a bit of an energy vampire yourself. After you have allowed yourself to be drained by an energy vampire, do you end up draining another person? Does your only attention come from negative things?

The harsh truth is that you must be on the same vibrational level as an energy vampire to attract them. Your core beliefs and thoughts are what create these vibrations. The emotions you experience are an indication of the vibration you have.

The good news is, you can prevent this from happening. But first, let's look at how you can identify energy vampires.

Identifying Energy Vampires

As I stated above psychopaths are energy vampires, but they aren't necessarily the most common ones that you might encounter. The best way to identify vampires you are in contact with is to think of the people who came to mind while you were reading the first part of this chapter.

Not everyone that exhibits narcissistic traits or who like being the center of attention are energy vampires. There are some that recognize what they are doing, and if you say something, they will stop. However, the real energy vampires are addicted to this kind of behavior. Many energy vampires may have inherited their traits from a parent and they are completely unaware of how they affect others. The following are the six main types of energy vampires:

1. Martyr or Victim Vampire

These vampires prey off of your guilt. They believe that they are at the mercy of the world and feel they suffer mainly because of other people, instead of taking responsibility for their life. They will continually emotionally blackmail, manipulate, and blame others. Their destructive behavior is typically caused by their low self-esteem. Without constantly getting signs of approval, love, and thanks, these vampires will feel unacceptable and unworthy, which they will try to fix by making the empath feel guilty and sucking away their empathy.

2. Narcissist Vampire

This type of vampire has no capacity for empathy or any genuine interest in others. They unconsciously carry the philosophy of "Me first, you second." They constantly expect you to place them first in your life, do what they say, and feed their egos. They will manipulate you with charm but will end up stabbing you in the back. If there is a narcissist vampire in your life, you could end up feeling extremely disempowered because you are crushed under their limelight.

3. Dominator Vampire

These vampires love to feel superior and alpha. Because of their insecurities of being wrong or weak, these vampires have to overcompensate by intimidating you. They are loud-mouthed people who have strong beliefs and black and white perceptions of the world. They tend to be bigoted, sexist, or racist.

4. Melodramatic Vampire

This type of vampire thrives on creating problems. Their need for creating drama typically comes from underlying emptiness. They love to seek out crisis because it gives them the chance to feel victimized, avoidance of real issues, and an exaggerated sense of self-importance. Another reason they like creating drama is that those negative emotions are addictive.

5. Judgmental Vampire

Because these people have very low self-esteem, they love to pick on others. The way they treat people is a reflection of how they treat their own self. They love to prey on insecurities and bolstering their own egos by making others feel ashamed, pathetic, or small.

6. Innocent Vampire

All energy vampires aren't malicious, just like with innocent vampires. These can be helpless types of people who actually need help like children or friends that tend to rely on you too much. It's good when you help people you care about, but they also need to be taught how to be self-sufficient. Playing the rock in their life will erode away your energy. This means you won't have the energy for yourself.

Here are a few more traits of energy vampires, just in case you need some more clarifying facts.

1. They drain you emotionally and physically so that you can't care for yourself.

Being around these toxic people is like being anchored down in tar. It affects you on a physiological and psychological level. The entire body is affected. You may have ailments that seem to come out of thin air.

2. When you aren't around them, you could still feel their effects.

You could find yourself stewing over odd things that they said or mean things they did. You will probably feel emotionally exhausted by their craziness, their need to cause problems, or their disrespect for your basic rights and needs. Severe anxiety is often something an empath will go through when they have been around an energy vampire.

3. You feel more energetic when you are away from them for a few days or weeks.

Once you remove yourself from them, it will give you time to psychologically reset so that you are more productive, lighter, and happier. It will feel like a great weight has been removed.

4. Try to come to a simple solution with them will leave you confused and upset.

You find that you have to explain basic human integrity, fairness, and decency to them. They won't give you straight answers and they won't view you as a person.

5. They act like a needle shoved in a balloon and their actions will cause you to questions your toxicity.

Whenever you feel confident, self-assured, and joyful, they will do their best to burst your bubble with criticism and put-downs. The longer you are around them, the more you may pick up their habits.

6. There will never be any reciprocity. You are there to fulfill their needs and that's it.

They are one-sided creatures. As an empath, you will give everything and they love to take it from you. Conversations will focus on them and they are the only important person. They make decisions without considering how you might feel.

7. They down you and they take a lot of pleasure in ruining your life.

Those who are higher on the narcissistic spectrum will be pathologically envious of the people they hurt. They become jealous when they see them successful and thriving. They covet everything you have. Instead of celebrating what you achieve, they try to diminish it. They will sometimes go so far as to come up with schemes or petty ploys.

Protect Yourself

You've just learned a lot about the energy vampire and while you may know how to identify them, you may still struggle to figure out if you have been affected by them. The following will help you tell if you have been the subject of an energy vampire's attack:

- A feeling that your aura is leaking or declining is the most common symptom of a psychic attack.

- Wooziness and exhaustion are both common symptoms of an attack.

- Lack of energy.

- Muscle tension.

- Chronic headaches.

- A constant weariness and low energy levels.

- Chronic impatience, irritation, and hypertension.

- Physical ailments like the flu, cold, or other such illnesses.

As an empath, it's crucial that you know how to protect yourself against these types of people. No matter how hard you work, these types of people will still pop up in your life every now and then.

1. Commit to the things that make you happy.

Do whatever you can to increase your vibrations so high that you won't be able to be a tool for an energy vampire. Don't live your life based on what other people expect of you. Meet your own needs and set boundaries. Saying no isn't you being mean. Being a good person is not determined by how much you sacrifice.

2. Match your vibrations to the kinds of people you want to connect with.

If you want to be around people who are well adjusted, competent, and respectful, you have to project those qualities. Remove your negative core beliefs that you hold about yourself that causes vampires to come into your life. Transmute those beliefs into something positive so that others will be attracted to you.

3. Understand that Source is an infinite house of energy.

Everybody has access to their own stream of Source Energy. It is impossible to give away all of your energy or to have it taken away. Energy vampires will cause you to experience negative thoughts that can cause you to lose your connection with your Source. When this is restricted, you will start to feel depressed, confused, exhausted, and so on.

4. Make it a priority to feel good.

Get your energy flowing by doing the types of things that you love that make you energized. You must love yourself so much that you can't act like the people who exhaust you and bring you down. You deserve to have a respectful and reciprocal relationship without feeling as if you must provide and serve all of your life force.

5. Understand that they are real.

Empaths are bad to think that everybody is good and will stick to bad relationships for a lot longer than they need to by creating excuses for the other person. Understanding that there are those out there who aren't good is going to help you protect yourself.

6. Follow your gut.

Empaths are extremely intuitive. After you have been around a vampire, this ability will sometimes wan. One way to gain back your gut is to journal. Make sure that you pay attention to the things your body says about others.

7. Say no.

This is the number one way to protect yourself. This will minimize the interactions you have with these people. You must know how to turn people down. This is going to take some practice. If you aren't able to say no, try to say something like "I'll get back to you." The most important thing is to stop saying yes automatically.

8. Find some support.

It's important that you find support once you fully understand your gift. This isn't just a good friend. This means finding a therapist who specializes in this type of problem. There are even some recovery groups.

9. Cut them out of your life if you can.

If you aren't constantly around them, then remove all contact. If you aren't able to, then try to cut out as much communication as you possibly can. If it is an ex-spouse with whom you share children, only text them when you communicate instead of talking in person.

10. Come up with strong boundaries.

Figure out the activities that you are able to handle with them. You might be able to handle them when you are in public places, but you don't want to be left alone with them in your house. It also helps to set beginning and end times.

11. Be the wet blanket.

Don't do things that will entertain them. This will make sure that they can't access your energy. Don't give them the response that they want and they will lose interest.

12. Differentiate between dumping and venting.

Everybody needs to voice their frustrations every now and then. Energy vampires love to dump their negative feelings, annoyances, irritations, bad days, and frustrations to everybody around them. People who vent know what role they played in their problem and want to find a solution. Dumping is mainly an unintelligible rant.

13. Keep yourself from overreacting.

Do whatever it takes for you to remain cool, calm, and collected around these types of people. Losing your cool is only going to give them what they were looking to get.

Chapter 9: Problems that Empathy can Cause

Because of all the energy that empaths take in, there is going to be some negative side effects. These can manifest into actual physical ailments. Empaths could experience a sudden onset of chronic fatigue because of a large crash in their energy level.

This is caused by a variety of emotional responsibilities since empaths leak their own energy when they can't stay in the present, balanced, grounded, and consciously aware.

Empaths often feel drained when they have been around people because these interactions can create emotional exhaustion. Empaths need a lot of alone time to be able to recharge their emotional batteries and retreat from society.

Our thoughts, feelings, and emotions can wreak havoc on the internal systems of an empath. This can cause devastating consequences that can leave them feeling debilitated. When empaths don't have space where they can quiet their minds, they can become overactive at night. This prevents them from being able to relax and get to sleep.

Their hyperactive mind will cause them to feel fatigued by the constant bombardment of stimuli. This doesn't let them replenish, recharge, and rest. This causes them to have erratic sleep patterns. Some days they might require ten or more hours of sleep, where other nights they might only need one or two.

Emotional feelings that are linked to memories could cause an empath to feel emotions like panic, paranoia, resentment, anxiety, and fear, so their brains become convinced they are under an actual threat. Therefore, the brain will signal the adrenal glands to produce hormones and this releases a surge of energy.

When empaths are exposed to intense of prolonged stress or anxiety, or they have an unhealthy lifestyle like a general life crisis, stressful family situations, stressful relationships, poor diet, substance abuse, overworking, or too little or too much sleep, they put a lot of demand on their adrenal glands.

These endocrine glands are the size of a walnut and shaped like a kidney. They are located just above the kidneys. They are great when you are under stress, but when they get over-stimulated, they will continue to produce energy which can leave the empath permanently wired and on high alert. In the end, they become burned out and malfunction.

When the adrenal gland is working properly, you might feel continuously fatigued, overwhelmed, anxious, rundown, dizzy, and irritable. You might experience high or low blood sugar, sugar or salt cravings, heart palpitations, and you might find it hard to deal with stressful situations.

During sleep, cortisol levels, which are produced by the adrenal glands, will naturally rise and peak a few hours before you get up. This is meant to give us a good start to our day. This is known as the circadian rhythm.

If you have exhausted adrenal glands, you might wake up feeling tired, even if you slept through the entire night. You might even feel drowsy during the majority of the day, but then cortisol peaks during the late evening and it makes it hard for you to go to sleep.

It will take some time for your adrenal glands to wear down, so it takes just as long to fully repair them. There are changes, though, that can have an immediate effect. The most important thing to do is make sure you listen to your body and pay close attention to the way you feel.

In order to keep your adrenal glands nourished and to avoid adrenal fatigue, you can eat a nutritional, organic, and well-balanced diet that has lots of protein and plenty of vitamins A, B, and C. Be sure that you are giving your body plenty of time to absorb these nutrients before you do any type of physical activity. It is also important that you stay away from drinking a lot of alcohol and reduce or get rid of refined salt, caffeine, and refined sugar intake.

By creating some security, getting lots of sleep, being optimistic, finding inner peace, stability, and joy will help you rebalance your adrenal glands. Just the thought of going to bed could cause some anxiety if we think we are going to be awake for hours, drifting in and out of sleep, but never reaching that much-needed delta state.

Meditation can help empaths to focus on their body so that they are aware of all sensations that are happening and it could help them soothe and calm their mind so they don't continue to repeat negative thought through their brain that is going to cause a chemical reaction.

Spending time with family and friends or going to social outing could also help re-regulate their cortisol levels. This is because they are known to increase when they spend a long time by themselves. This means that they will feel separated, lonely, and isolated. If an empath feels content in their own company, they will feel balanced and their cortisol levels won't become an issue.

Their exercise and diet program could also add stress to their adrenal glands. If they push their bodies too much, there might be too much demand on their adrenal glands. This could cause them to produce too much of the stress-related hormones.

Intense workout, skipping meals, and eating junk foods could cause the adrenal glands to become overworked. If an empath has food allergies, this could put even more stress on their glands, so it is important for them to pay attention to the food intolerances they have.

If the adrenal glands get fatigued, you might wake up during the night on high alert from a dream that was very stimulating. This will just add to your overanxious state.

Sleepless nights are more common when you endure anxious and stressful periods because even if you can go to sleep, you might wake up during the night feeling the adrenaline coursing through your veins but not knowing why. These sleep disturbances are closely linked to biochemical reactions because of high levels of stress hormones through the body at around two to four AM. This spike in your hormones will dramatically affect your ability to stay calm, which is the reason why your sleep gets interrupted.

This could be fixed through making up some magical and therapeutic potions with unrefined salt and organic honey. It is also helpful to have a Himalayan salt lamp by your bed. This will get rid of positive ions in the environment and replace them with negative ions, which mimics the balance in nature. It will also help to get rid of electric smog that your electronic devices cause so that the air remains clear. This means you will have improved air circulation and be able to breathe better.

Chapter 10: How to Handle Empathy in Your Life

Everyone would love to find their soul mate, have close friends and connect to their family. However, empathic people often struggle in this area for many reasons. Romance is very hard for an empath.

An empathic person has a tendency to have a hard time when finding romance. It is interesting when you know two empaths who each have mental scars get together. They have a very hard time getting past feeling the other's hidden issues and pains.

They might spend hours arguing with the other about how they know something is wrong just to have the other say they knew their partner was upset.

The real problems are in these things:

1. Empaths can scare the crap out of you.

It could be exciting, especially if you are an empath to meet another empath that could potentially be your romantic partner. You would think they could express their feelings better than people who aren't empaths. They do because they know their feelings, unlike normal people who like to second guess their feelings. This means, it might be weeks into your relationships and they might tell you "I love you." Nothing will be able to change an empaths mind about how they feel. This could ruin the relationship at times.

2. Inconsistency could create more struggles.

Empaths don't like it when what people say don't match what they do or what they feel because empaths can pick up on all this stuff. It is tough on them when they have to call out their family, friends, and partners. This can become very rough if they are living in close quarters with loved ones. Empaths can pick up on every little smudge on the surface of honesty.

3. Empaths can be moody.

This is hard for relationships and friendships. Due to their strong emotions, things can get out of control at times. Most of the time, the feelings that go through an empath's body won't be their own. The main problem is they might have absorbed too much energy from their loved one. This might wind up being sent back to the original owner of that particular emotion. It is very unfair that the empath will get blamed for this, but this is how it usually works out.

4. Empaths can pick up on complacency.

You know how some relationships eventually reach a plateau? Empaths can sense this before it happens. Every new relationship is going to reach a point where things taper off and settle. This isn't a bad thing. It just means the relationship has leveled out.

An empath will notice and might begin to panic. They might begin stirring up trouble just to get some intensity back into the relationship. If their partner can't sense this, they might think the empath is being very strange. In reality, it is nothing but a gift that has gone awry.

5. Empaths need their own space but don't like to be alone, either.

This is such a lovely conundrum, isn't it? It might seem strange, but if you analyze it the right way, it does make sense. Empaths love being in love and they love to spend time with their partner. They also need to have a space of their own when they need it. They will be more emotional when they don't have their personal time. They need to have time to recuperate and energize themselves.

6. Empaths won't give up.

Empaths will not break up, divorce, or dissolve a romantic relationship or any relationship for that matter. It doesn't matter if this is their best option. Empathic people will always see the potential in other people because they can feel the frustration in the relationship. This struggle happens when an empath is married to someone who is not in touch with their feelings and the word divorce comes up in conversation. The empath will want to hold things together no matter what. Imagine that there is a person more compatible for the empath but they won't know it because they are going to continue to try to revive what they have already lost.

7. They never get taken seriously.

This is the largest problem for any relationship an empath has whether it is romantic or not. They are going to have ideas that are going to sound far-fetched but if they can be given the benefit of the doubt, they will convince people just how much their words mean. This is usually a struggle for many relationships because most people just say things and will only do them about 40 percent of the time.

People are used to just believing less than half of what others say, especially in a close relationship. The thing is, empaths will tell you they can do something and can actually do it. This is why it hurts so much when other people don't believe them.

It is important that the empaths' friends, family, and romantic partners take them seriously. Empaths are the most real people out there and that is why they usually struggle in their relationships.

Relationship Sabotage

As you might have figured out by now, empaths are prone to having more relationship problems than normal people do. They also respond to these problems differently and in unusual ways. These ways are not always healthy. Here is a list of different ways an empath might sabotage their relationship.

- They won't stop expressing their own needs.

Empaths get so focused on making their partner happy that they end up neglecting their own self. An empath is very prone to forget how important it is for them to express their needs and making sure they get met. This can cause things to happen that will harm the relationship. The empath begins to feel neglected and their partner isn't going to understand.

- They compromise boundaries without being asked to.

Empaths will often feel their partner's needs in such a profound way that they decide to give into them in ways that will end up hurting them. They might choose to negate a boundary that their partner didn't ask them to cross. When they make this decision without letting their partner know, the empath is opening themselves up to anger and resentment. Their partner won't understand what happened. They will become confused and frustrated because of it.

- They don't take care of themselves.

Because empaths are so concerned with other people's emotional well-being, they will often neglect themselves. When they get too focused on another person, they will sometimes neglect the things that make them who they are. This might mean that they spend less time with their friends, less energy for things they like to do, and less focus on their work that they find meaningful. This can cause their self-esteem and happiness to suffer.

- Important problems get solved in their head.

It is common for an empath to keep a running dialogue in their head and they will take on both sides of the argument. The empath will often resolve the issue in their head and they won't even bring up the issue. This might get rid of the problem, but it could just as easily create new ones. It is very unfair to their partner who isn't even aware that there is a conflict. It robs them of autonomy, their chance to defend their self, and the opportunity to understand the empaths viewpoint.

Be sure that if you are an empath you don't become prey to your own devices. Try to find these behaviors and fight them so you can create a healthy relationship.

Empathy at Work

Studies have been done and found out that people who work together can "catch" another's emotions. This means that one person's panic could spread through the office like flu. This will lower productivity and morale.

The opposite could also be true and happiness might build in the workplace. This will result in improved performance, satisfaction, and cooperation.

The problem for empaths is that these feelings are stronger. These feeling are amplified in them. The good thing is, though, empaths are also able to benefit from positivity that runs through the office. The hard thing happens when they pick up on illnesses and negative emotions.

Everyone is going to have bad days. Unfortunately for empaths, a bad day for one co-worker might mean a bad day for them, too. Many offices now are "open concept." This means that desks don't have walls separating them or they are made up of cubicles with glass partitions. This means that everyone uses the same space. People are able to hear all the candy wrappers being opened, someone snapping their gum, laughing, humming, blowing noses, gossiping, talking, complaining, and coughing. You are able to smell everyone's perfume, what they ate for lunch, and you can see everyone moving around. This puts you on sensory overload. Having very little privacy makes an empath vulnerable to their co-worker's stress.

But there are some pretty effective solutions. Shopify asked their employees about this and discovered that there was a balance between extroverts and introverts. They had office designers modify the workplace to accommodate each group. Some of the sections were more interactive and noisier.

Then there were other offices that with couches that had high backs that they could move into the corner to create some privacy and they made designated rooms that looked like libraries for quiet work. This new design element offered the introverts more peacefulness and space to work. Because of this design, they weren't as exposed to the stress of their office-mates.

Empaths also have to deal with the emotions of their clients, even when they are just talking on the phone. To deal with this problem, the following are some ways to create boundaries for your energy at work.

- If you work in a chaotic office, fill the edges of your workspace with happy photos and plants to make a psychological barrier. You could also use sacred objects or healings stones to create a boundary for your energy.

- Take breaks or take a few minutes outside to get a reprieve from the noise.

- If you are allowed to, use noise-canceling headphones so you can muffle out some of the noise from your surrounding areas.

- It might help to visualize a golden light enveloping your complete workstation that will repel any negativity and lets positive energy in.

Any of these techniques are going to help you create a wall of protection so you don't fall prey to the emotions of the people you work with.

Chapter 11: Become More Self-Aware

In order to understand other people, we have to understand ourselves. We need to teach people that we are all made up of different personalities like our inner critic or our happy voice. Our goal is to recognize all the parts of our personalities to become more aware of our patterns and tendencies. This helps us navigate relationships and the way we connect with others.

When we can improve the different parts of our personalities, we also improve the ability to understand other people's mental states. This is called empathy or theory of mind.

Empathy and self-awareness are intimately connected. When we get more aware of what makes us the person we are, we can understand the difference between others and ourselves and what makes them the person they are.

It isn't surprising to know that empathy and self-awareness are the two main characteristics behind emotional intelligence. Empathy is being aware of others and its counterpart is self-awareness.

Once you become aware of yourself, you will become aware of others. The self will be clearer and you will start to see the ways you are different and similar to others in the way you feel and think.

This is an important part of empathy, it isn't about finding ways you are like others but seeing the ways you are different. You can easily empathize with other people when you think they are just like you. It isn't trying to understand their perspective, it is just projecting your perspective onto them.

You might be an introvert but you understand that everybody isn't going to be just like you. When you meet a person who is more extroverted, it shouldn't surprise or frustrate you. Just realize that you both have different tendencies and personalities and keep this in mind when you are around them.

There are ways you can start to improve your self-awareness that you can begin right now:

- Meditation

This is the best way to improve self-awareness. If you are a beginner, just learning how to breathe will help you tremendously. Doing breathing meditation is a wonderful way to become aware of your feelings and thoughts as you begin to accept them without judgment. Meditation can teach you how you can look at your surroundings and yourself without having to react. It is a wonderful way to self-regulate. This is another aspect of emotional intelligence.

- Personality Quizzes

If you can learn more about your personality, it will help you understand how your mind works and how it is different from other people. There are free surveys that will help you get a better understanding of the real you. These will show you different traits such as introversion, extraversion, big picture, and detail oriented. Your score on these quizzes will bring some insight into the type of personality you have.

- Contemplation

Meditation helps you watch your feelings and thoughts. Contemplation helps you analyze your mind and learn about your thought process. Taking 10 to 15 minutes every day to sit down and analyze your thoughts and beliefs is a great way to be aware of the way your mind works.

- Role-playing

One way to figure out more about you is to pretend to be someone else. When you practice this, it might reveal some hidden aspects of yourself that you aren't aware of. When you try to be someone who is very different than you, it will show you what will or won't fit into your personality.

- Ask Friends

Many times our family and friends know more about us than we do. Some personality traits get so deeply ingrained that we just take them for granted. A good way to increase your self-awareness is to ask a friend. Ask them to describe you as a person. This might reveal some patterns that they see in us that we can't see for ourselves. Friends are good at seeing our extroversion, creativity, and intelligence.

These are great ways to begin improving our self-awareness. Will we ever be able to completely know ourselves? That is one question that doesn't have an answer. We are complicated beings and it might be possible to never totally grasp who we really are.

If we can actively build self-awareness, it will help you improve yourself and your ability to connect with others in a meaningful and genuine way.

Remember how important self-awareness is and try some of the exercises above to start improving it.

Chapter 12: Normalizing, Fine Tuning and Maintaining Your Gift

Understanding your gift is one thing, embracing it and helping it grow is another. It's important that you feel comfortable and normal with your gift because it makes you who you are. The exercises in this chapter will help you to fine-tune your abilities so that you can be the best empath possible.

- Challenge yourself – Undertake some challenging experiences which will push you past your comfort zone. Try learning something new like a foreign language, hobby, or instrument. Create a new competency. Doing this is going to humble you and humility is important for enabling empathy.

- Move outside of your normal environment – Travel, especially to a place with new cultures. This will help you to appreciate others.

- Receive feedback – Ask your colleagues, family, and friends for feedback about your relationship skills and then check in with them every now and then.

- Get to know your heart and not just your head – Read books that explore personal emotions and relationships. This has been proven to help improve the empathy of new doctors.

- Take a moment to walk in somebody else's shoes – Talk with other people about what it is like to be them. Ask about their concerns and issues and how they view experiences that you both have experienced.

- Look at your biases – Everybody has hidden and not-so-hidden biases that can interfere with their ability to empathize. These tend to be centered on visible factors like gender, age, and race. Don't believe you have any sort of biases? Think again, everybody does.

- Create some curiosity – What are you able to learn from some colleagues who are "inexperienced?" What might will you be able to learn from a client you have claimed is "narrow?" People who are curious will ask a lot of questions which leads them to create a stronger understanding of those around them.

- Ask questions – Make sure that you have some questions to ask when you are having a conversation.

- Take a class – There are online courses for empaths that can help you to practice your skills and nurture your abilities.

- Talk with an expert – Find a person who you think has strong empathy skills. Ask them how they have improved their abilities.

- Expand your imagination – When you are working to see things from another's point of view, try putting together everything that you know about them and create an inner picture. Based on the picture you have created, try to see what the world looks like through their eyes.

- Learn the art of listening – The more actively you listen which means you hear what they say without judging or preparing what you are going to say, the more you will learn about their side. In order to listen actively, you have to turn off your "internal judge" when a person is talking.

Controlling Emotions

Overactive empathy happens when you open up to the emotions of others, but you aren't able to return to normal. This means you are left out there to absorb other people's stuff. When you are in social gatherings, you are able to sense everything that other's feel and think.

This can lead to self-neglect, people pleasing, and self-sacrifice. This is something that many empaths will struggle with. If you find yourself experiencing overactive empathy, it's important that you control the emotions and become more centered. To control your emotions, all you need are these tips:

1. Notice your feelings

Tune back into what are your real feelings. You have to check, at the very least once a day with yourself to see how you feel. Keep a log that you fill in before bed that explains the emotions you went through that day. When somebody asks you for a favor, before saying yes, check with yourself to see how you feel. Don't respond to only their needs. Center yourself so that you know how you feel about the task.

2. Talk to your source to remove energies you don't need

If you start to feel emotionally overwhelmed or you feel like you have lost yourself, take three deep breaths and say this prayer:

"I call upon Source/God to clear my energy field of all energies that are not serving me. So it is."

You can even come up with your own prayer if you want. There's no need for it to be long or complicated. This is a very powerful clearing technique.

3. Allow yourself to enjoy you

The majority of empaths rarely have fun when they have to interact with others. They go into situations with the belief that they have to help those who are not happy or well. They feel responsible and dutiful for the people's feelings.

To fix this, focus on trying to have fun in how you interact. If you find that you aren't into a conversation with somebody, then don't engage with them. If the person you are talking to is draining you, pull back. Your enjoyment should be put first when in a social gathering. Don't focus so much on. This might sound selfish, but empaths have to establish boundaries to control their emotions.

Chapter 13: Keeping Out Unwanted Emotions

While being an empath is a great skill, what do you do if you start getting overwhelmed by other's negative emotions? The good news is that there are ways to stop absorbing the feelings of other people while still being a good empath.

Being empathic is normal for many humans, especially empaths. Empathy can be found in all animals that are social like mice and primates. The majority of people evolve their empathy from parental instincts. All parents, animal or human, will tune into their children so that they bond with them and can figure out when they are in distress. This is the reason why a lot of adults don't like to hear a baby cry or we start laughing when a baby giggles. Empathy is why we sneeze or yawn when somebody else does it. We also tend to mimic the facial expressions and body language of others. The brain is made that way.

Not only can an empath catch a person's yawn, they actually catch their moods. This can be great when your friend is happy and they give you a mood boost. But it gets exhausting when your boss's anxiety, partner's stress, co-worker's grief, or the crankiness of the teenager at the McDonalds infects you. Secondhand stress or anger is like secondhand smoke.

With growing research, it's easy to notice how negativity caught from each other can impact a person's educational and business outcome. It can also impact the empath on a cellular level and if not handled, it can shorten their lifespan. There are some hotels that have noticed the problem with secondhand stress and have started to create "no venting" zones where the employees aren't allowed to vent around customers. If an empath goes to the doctor and feels the nurse seething with anger, they are likely to catch the anger and it could end up affecting the doctor's visit.

What can we do about this without isolating our self from society altogether and live as a hermit? This is going to take boundaries and a change in your perspective to make sure you stay protected from the emotions of others.

1. Label their feelings

When you are able to label another person's emotions, it will create some distance between you and the emotion. It will give you some time to reflect so that you can deal with it and figure out how to react. It will help you to deal with emotions that are negative. It will help you if you have to respond to your child's meltdown. By saying "so and so" is feeling "this way," you state that they are feeling that way and you aren't. Language will create a barrier between your thoughts and feelings and will lessen the strength of the emotions.

2. Limit social media and negativity

We no longer only deal with information overload, we have to face emotional overload. This can be stressful for the empath. You click into Facebook and you are bombarded with your friend's emotions of hungry, mad, sad, and any other emotion you can think of. Twitter is another home for extreme emotions. When some form of tragedy strikes and the story hits the news, everybody' emotions will get added to yours. You are now more connected to people than ever before whether you realize it or not. Those people on social media will influence you daily.

You have to learn how to be selective with your exposure to news media and social media. Remove friends who always post horrible passive-aggressive things that are aimed at people they hate. If you need a break from the real news, try reading The Onion for some satirical things. Never, EVER, read comments. They are the quickest way to get sucked down an emotional rabbit hole.

3. Create limits

If you surround yourself with chronic complainers or negative people, you will have to learn how to deflect their negativity. You must eliminate or reduce the time you spend around them. This is going to be hard if you work in a toxic environment. If your family tends to constantly stress, even though they are family, you must limit the amount of time you spend around them. You may discover that you have to break off friendships that you've had since grade school. You can't help anybody if your emotions are constantly being sabotaged. It may be hard to realize this, but after you move away and leave all of this negativity behind, your life is going to get calmer.

4. Create a wall of positivity

There is no way to block out all negative emotions, but you can also increase positive ones. It always sounds corny when you are told to practice positivity and gratitude, but if you are able to make it a part of your everyday life, your happiness is going to increase. Try some gratitude when you end up crying over somebody else's hurt. This can also work if you see something on television that is upsetting. This will help you to remember and feel all of the good times in your life and in the world even though you are experiencing negativity.

If you are able to build up a wall of immunity, it is going to help you take care of your wellbeing and self-esteem. The best buffer you can have against other's stress is to have a strong and stable self-esteem. If your self-esteem is high, you are going to be able to handle situations more easily. When you notice that you are being hindered by the moods of others, take a moment and to remind yourself that things are great and that you can handle it. Exercise is another great way to improve your self-esteem because the brain will make a record of the times that you exercise by releasing endorphins.

Before you face a stressful moment, give yourself a shot of gratitude. Before you start your day, the first thing you should do is think of three things that you are grateful of. Here are five other things that you can do each day to boost your brain against negativity:

- o Two-minute meditation

- o 30 minutes of cardio

- o Two minutes writing down positive experiences

- o Write down a few things you are grateful for

- o Send a friend an email praising them for what they accomplished

Make sure you spend a lot of time that is positive and joyful. This doesn't mean everybody must be uplifting 24 hours a day seven days a week. Just being around a person who tends to generally be happy is going to give you a boost for your positivity wall. Your favorite song or the sound of a child's laughter can boost your mood if you are having a really bad day.

5. Change to compassion

Learning how to change your empathy into compassion is a great technique. Compassion is very different than empathy. Different parts of the brain are triggered when you share another person's pain or if you respond to their suffering.

Figuring out the difference between the two is important. As an empath, you are constantly feeling another person's pain and suffering. These moments can be so intense that it creates real distress inside of you. But if you can learn to feel compassion for the person, you won't take in as much of their energy. You will feel concerned for them and you will feel more motivated to help them.

Using techniques such as meditation will enforce a loving kindness that will help your brain to shift your empathy into compassion. Basically, you have to learn the art of detached attachment.

6. Create lighter discussion

There are some negative attitudes that get triggered by seemingly harmless topics. Your friend could turn into a toxic self-victimizer when you start talking about their job. No matter what is said, they constantly complain about everything and when you try to add in some positive things, they ignore them completely and spews out more negativity. This will become a conversation dampener.

When you find yourself in a moment like this and the person you are conversing with is stuck on something that is bringing you down, realize that those negative feelings are probably deeply rooted. The best thing that you could do is to bring up a new topic that can lighten the mood. Bring up things like funny memories, friendships, success stories, and other types of happy news that can create a lighter conversation. Stick to things that they feel positive about.

    7. Release the want to change a person's negative tendencies

Some people can be helped by creating a good example for them, others you can't. When you can recognize the difference, it'll help maintain your equilibrium. Don't let energy vampires, emotional blackmailers, and manipulators control you by trying to control something you can't, which are other people's behaviors.

That said, if there is a behavior that somebody you love has that you hope will change, it likely won't. If you are in desperate need for them to change, be honest with them and lay all your cards out so that they know how and why you feel that way.

For the most part, you won't be able to change people and you need to quit trying. You either have to accept who they are or you have to live without them. This may sound harsh, but really it isn't. When you try to change a person, they will resist and stay exactly the same, but when you don't try to change them and you support them, they may gradually change. What changes the most is the way that you view them.

Chapter 14: Healing

You've likely started to wonder if being an empath is a blessing or a curse. Ask any empath, they may say it's a curse. The extreme empaths could tell you it's a death sentence. If some are able to see it as a gift, why do so many hate it? Do empaths really have a purpose?

Most intuitive is an empath to a certain degree. If they weren't, then they wouldn't be able to tap into the energy of other people or feel their spirit. Let's talk about those who don't only feel anxieties, emotions, and illnesses of others but they manifest the feelings as their own.

If you have run across a person who is always in some form of pain, feels tired all the time, and has some unexplained illnesses, these are likely empaths. These people aren't hypochondriacs. They haven't been able to figure out how to deal with their abilities. Empaths will often get sick and tired faster than the average person. This is because they consume a lot of bad energies and don't realize it. They allow the energy to build in them until it becomes a physical condition. It could be lethargy, illness, or anxiety.

If you notice that you are experiencing anxiety or depression, it could be other people's energies and emotions. It's important that you figure out a way of getting rid of the old energy, reset yourself, and learn the best way to protect yourself from the energy of others. Working with a coach could be helpful since they can help you learn specific techniques and lessons that you can continue to use throughout your life.

While there may be times where being an empath feels like a curse, but it is honestly a gift. Once you have figured out the best way to use your gift, you find that you can help a lot of other people.

Empaths make perfect healers. They are able to sense the pain in others and can help them to heal it. Most people don't even realize where their emotional pain is resonating from, empaths can help. They have the ability to sense out the bad energy so why not use it? Empaths are also great reiki practitioners, truth-seers, and spiritual coaches.

Are you an empath, but you're not interested in working in the spiritual world? That's fine. They are also perfect as nurses, firemen, hospice caregivers, and acupuncturists. These are all healing fields that are great for the empath.

Empaths are the perfect healers because they are able to feel things on such a deep level. It probably sounds crazy to be an empath and work in areas that put you close to other's energy, but that's what you were born to do.

You will find that you take in others energy, but there are plenty of ways to release it without allowing it to boil under the surface, which will turn into anxiety or illness. It's important that you manage your gift and in doing so, you will improve your life. Once you have figured out how to identify your emotions and energy and you know how to release it, everything will become easier and you will be able to align with your purpose. You will become the healer you were meant to be.

A lot of empaths will try to hide away from the world. This may sound good in theory, but it's not teaching them how to handle energy. With time empaths can learn a lot of healing techniques so that they can live a completely full life.

There is going to be a shift when you focus on being all that you can be instead of just trying to survive. This is when you will allow yourself to awaken fully. You will shift from feeling as if it's a curse and embrace it. Let's take a look at how you can learn how to release past experiences and clean out what isn't serving you so that you can heal. Anybody can use these techniques, empath or not, to create a life change. The point is to realize that you have to start where you are. You aren't trying to create a new version of yourself. This will be a disservice to any real work that you try. You have to be transparent with yourself and this will take a lot of courage, but it is the most important step.

You can and should put your needs first. This may sound like it goes against what an empath is, but this has to be done from the very start. It's important to understand that everything in the Universe is energy and that everything is connected. Many of these techniques are going to work with the spiritual realm and energy. As long as you keep your mind open, everything will work. There are a lot of steps along your path to healing. It will take some time before you can settle into a rhythm that will feel right and safe. Everybody can heal misalignments and diseases that are inside us with intention, open minds, imagination, and a warm heart.

Everything is just a part of the ritual that you will use to put yourself in a state of being so that your inner healer is able to help others. You will need to trust the unknown for these practices to work. They will take some magic, creativity, imagination, and faith.

Most empaths, unfortunately, have suffered at the hands of somebody that they loved deeply. From years of unmet childhood needs, not being understood, a lot of empaths suffer from distrust and low self-esteem. They've suffered rejection or ridicules because they are sensitive and they could be defensive about it or they suppress their self completely. A lot of them will have trust issues that are so bad they can't even trust their self. They likely feel as if their own bodies and emotions betray them. People close to them may have abandoned them during moments of need. This will often create a pattern in their relationships where they try to find others who match that part. With practice, they will be able to figure out the reason behind abandoning their self when their emotions become too much.

The biggest shift is going to come when you realize that there is no need for you to sacrifice your happiness for somebody else. Once you understand that your feelings matter, that your emotions and thoughts matter, you will be able to come up with a way to handle overwhelming negative emotions. You could find yourself at a point in your life where it feels like caring for somebody means you must give them your last breath. You will likely neglect your needs to show those around you that you care. There is likely going to be times when people mistake your kindness for weakness.

In order for you to nurture your wholeness and happiness, you will need to learn how to express to others the things that don't serve your wellbeing.

You must stop doing the following:

- o People pleasing

- o Enabling behavior that is destructive

- o Doing other's work

- o Being a scapegoat for another's unresolved trauma

- o Spending time with others because you feel guilty

- o Providing a person energy who doesn't care about your time or feelings

- o Allowing yourself to be a victim

- o Being codependent

Empaths will face a lot of damage from narcissists. Since there is a constant barrage of emotions coming at the empath, there will likely be wounds created that can't heal. It may often seem impossible to deal with your issues while carrying other's baggage. We are going to look at a few ways to heal from your past and heal for the future.

As I mentioned earlier, most empaths were probably ridiculed or made fun of as a child. People didn't understand them, so they made fun. What some may see as small jokes carve a deep scar into an empath. All they want is to be accepted by people they care about, so when those they love criticize them for who they are, it hurts.

Oftentimes, an empath may not have faced being made fun of for their sensitivity, instead, they had a traumatic childhood in general. During childhood, they may have been surrounded by criminal behavior, mental illness, substance abuse, or violence. This then led to empathy.

Either way, scars have been made and those have to be healed. Luckily, there are several ways you can heal your childhood now to help you with your empathy.

1. Reframe

You can't change what happened, unfortunately, but you can control the way you experience it now. Instead of allowing yourself to respond in the same way you did when a disturbing incident pops in your mind, take a moment to pause and breathe. Then take a moment to reinterpret that memory. Ask, "How did this make me stronger?"

2. Get rid of shame

Unlike guilt or remorse, shame has nothing to do about feeling bad for what you did, instead, it's feeling bad for what you are. Shame kills your spirit. This is where feelings of undeserving, worthlessness, and unlovable come from. Oftentimes, childhood troubles will cause shame which you try to treat by making "psychic promises." These are things like say "I'll act like my parents so that they will treat me better." "If I get rid of my feelings, I won't have to experience the pain."

To keep these contracts from destroying you, figure out what promises you made and allow yourself to break them. Shame is a lie, don't listen to it. You are worthy of respect and love.

3. Let go of the pain

Research has found that people who write down their past traumas will heal faster. Take some time to write out letters to those who hurt you. Nobody ever has to see them, so you don't have to censor yourself. Let out all of your rages on that piece of paper. To take it a step further, burn the paper once you have written the letter. This will act like an even bigger release.

4. Stop regret

Having the repetition of "I should have..." and "If only..." statements will destroy your health and your peace of mind. To heal, you have to stop punishing yourself for previous mistakes. Forgive yourself, learn the lessons you need to, and resolve to perform differently in the future. Take a look back at regrettable things and recall who you were then. What did and didn't you know at that time? What choices did you have? By reviewing the scenario, you could discover that you did the best you could at that time.

5. From grief to gain

Emotional wounds are as real as physical wounds. To mend them, you will have to move through three phases of grief: shock/denial, anger/sadness/fear, and understanding/acceptance. Many people get stuck in the shock/denial phase. You can move past that stage and find yourself bogged down in chronic anger or fear. Either way, your healing isn't complete. No matter how long ago it was, you have to allow yourself to feel the emotions that you suppressed. Find ways to express those emotions so that you can move to phase three, understanding and acceptance.

6. Create gratitude

Gratitude is better than acceptance. No matter the things that happened to you, tell yourself that you have gifts that you should be thankful for. You could even find that you are grateful for your troubles because they have shaped you today.

7. Satisfying future

Living well is the best revenge. The best way to find peace with your past is to be the person you are meant to be. The grip of old perceptions and patterns can be strong to the point that you feel like a helpless victim. In fact, you are the creator of your life and a new scene can be started at any time.

8. Acceptance

This acceptance doesn't have to do with your past. Instead, once you have worked through your past, you must accept the fact that you are an empath. Quit wondering if you might be. Accept yourself for who you are. Empaths are beautiful people.

9. Own it

Once you have accepted the fact that you are an empath, allow it to be a part of you. Be proud and own your existence. It's believed that around one in 20 people is a true empath, so take pride in your sensitivities. This is the only way to make sure you quit feeling like you're a victim.

10. Meditate

Meditation is such an important thing for an empath. There are hundreds of different techniques that you can try. Find what works for you. Some people will use music or white noise. Others have to have complete silence. Explore different things and use what you like.

11. Love it

Now that you accept and own the fact that you're an empath, you now need to love it. You are special and unique. You are a blessing in other's lives. Other people are not a burden. Being an empath is only a single part of you. This isn't a condition that has to be treated.

12. Create boundaries

Boundaries are extremely crucial. View these boundaries as lines in the sand. Those in your life need to stay on their side. If they cross the line, you will be able to distance yourself. Be honest about these boundaries. They shouldn't be invisible. The hardest thing for an empath is getting rid of those people who don't respect their boundaries.

Important Truths

A person's energy will tell you more about them than their words will. As a child, you were likely quiet and shy. You wanted to watch people instead of getting involved. You probably picked up on nuances and undercurrents of thoughts and emotions.

Pain, people, energy, faces, sensations, words, feelings, and meaning — you are likely about to feel all of these. It could make you feel sick. When you learn that you're an empath, you will find a new door to healing and self-discovery. You will no longer be alone.

The following are eight important truths that you are going to discover as an empath:

1. You don't have to take on a person's pain.

As an empath, you can feel other's pain and you will internalize it. What you need to remember is that you can only do so much. You can guide others to help them as much as you can, but they have to help themselves in order to heal. An empath's nature will blind them to this fact. There are a lot of people who don't want to be fixed because they are comfortable in their misery.

2. Accept the pain, don't escape it.

This will allow you to release the energy in you. When you focus on trying to escape or repress pain, you will cause a cycle of suffering. Quit running and sit down and let yourself experience fatigue, hurt, confusion, and anger. This will allow you to let it go.

3. You could project your emotions on others.

As an empath, you have a bit of an escape hatch. It creates an opportunity to blame others. You soak up emotions like a sponge, but that doesn't mean you don't create experiences of your own. It is very easy for empaths to act the victim. It's harder to accept your happiness. You have to distinguish your feelings from other's feelings and sometimes there may not be a clear distinction.

4. Self-esteem is important for an empath.

Empaths with low self-esteem will suffer more than those who have a healthy self-esteem. This isn't always obvious. It's quite easy to blame feelings of hopelessness and worthlessness on the energy that you have absorbed. Once you realize you can create trust, respect, and love inside yourself, your suffering will stop.

5. Being an empath is different than having empathy.

Empathy and compassion are not the same. It doesn't mean you feel sorry for others and you want to help them out. Empathy is looking past what people say or do and understanding their values, feelings, beliefs, and situations. Having empathy is being able to understand people and walking in their shoes. Empathy is intellectual and emotional. Being an empath is an emotional, physical, and kinesthetic experience. You can share a person's feelings, but you might not understand it on a deeper level. Understanding the difference between empath and empathy will help you grow so that you can create empathy.

6. Shielding doesn't always help.

Shielding can help temporarily, but it won't help for long. Shielding means you are resisting the energy of other's and this only causes more pain and fear for you. Open yourself up to emotions instead of fighting them. Allow yourself to experience this and let them go. This will take practice.

7. Mindfulness and catharsis are great.

Incorporating catharsis into your life is important for releasing bad energy. Helpful forms of catharsis include journaling, jogging, writing, walking, and meditation. Singing, crying, laughing, dancing, and privately screaming can also help. You also need to learn how to tune into your body. This can help you to anchor yourself at the moment instead of getting lost in emotions and sensations.

8. Everybody can be an empath.

This doesn't mean it's something for you and a few other people. Empaths do have wonderful gifts. The real beauty comes from the fact that these gifts aren't limited to a few people. This form of sensitivity is a natural state. With conditioning, beliefs, and upbringings, many of us have lost touch with this state.

Clearing Emotions

Throughout this book, we have talked a lot about energy and emotions. You should be fully aware of the fact that you will absorb a lot of this no matter how hard you try to avoid it. It's a fact for the empath, so it's best to accept. That being said, it's important that you clear out these emotions from time to time. This is something that is called spiritual cleansing. This will help you to improve your gift as well as reduce the risk of negative side effects due to negative emotions. Let's dive right in.

1. Cut the cord

This is important for all empaths since you are great at creating relationships due to the fact that everybody loves you. The problem is, not all of your relationships are good for you and your energy can be sucked out.

The cords of relationships from the past can still exist even if the relationship has ended. You have to cut these cords. In order to do this, visualize the person you have had a relationship with and visualize a cord being sliced. Bless them and say "I release you into the light and love."

There are a lot of advanced techniques to cut the cord, but this is a very easy and simple one you can use. If you complicate it too much, you may find it harder to do.

2. Clear negative thoughts from your aura

Since your energy is constantly mingling with other's energy, sucking up their negative thoughts, you may form thoughts that won't serve your highest purpose. You need to be aware of thoughts that are automatic, repetitive, redundant, and negative.

Carry around a notebook and jot down the thoughts you experience during the day. It will be amazing to see how hard it will be to track thoughts. When you have positive thoughts, they will align with positive vibrations which create harmony, healing, and balance. Negative thoughts cause blockages and resistance.

To clear negativity, look back at your life to notice if you are pulling these bad situations to yourself. If you are, you are vibrating these things into alignment unconsciously. You need to notice your field of energy throughout the day, especially when you start feeling depressed or tired. This will allow you to find out if you have grabbed hold of or created negative thought-forms and then consciously release these.

Picture a silver light cleansing your energy of any thoughts that aren't helping you. This will only take about a minute and can be done multiple times during the day.

3. Smudge your environment and yourself

This is important if you really start to feel down, anxious, or sad. Smudging your environment and yourself helps to remove negative energy. This should be done often, especially when you have been in situations that cause you to feel out of synch. Smudging your house on a regular basis is important too so that the energy their stays fresh.

4. Connect with nature

Everybody who starts to feel overwhelmed, all they have to do is take some time to connect with nature. Nature will cleanse the negative emotions from you. Touch a tree and it will ground you and remove bad energies. Connecting with water, animals, flowers, and the land around you are the most soothing energy therapy. And it's completely free! Take a moment to sit in your yard, against a tree, or take a barefoot walk.

5. Draw, journal, art

Empaths are normally very artistic and love to express their talents. When they aren't feeling great, they will resist their artistic abilities because they require them to feel their feelings and this will cause pain. Art should be used as a form of emotional release that will help you to get yourself unstuck.

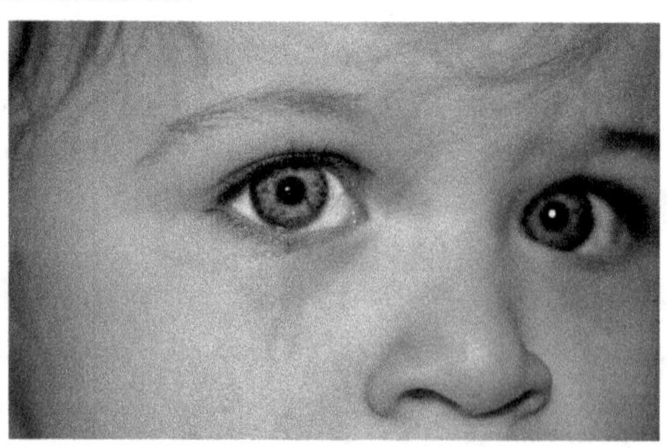

6. Cry

Empaths need to cry often to release emotions. Crying can cleanse your aura.

7. Sea salt bath

Sea salt draws out energy. Taking a warm bath in sea salt is great when you are feeling energetically overwhelmed. Add some essential oils to help release even more.

These are just a few ways to release emotions and you may find other ways that work better for you. What is important is that you take care of yourself and don't allow emotions to remain stagnant inside of you.

Chapter 15: How to Support a Young Empath

An empathic child will have a nervous system that reacts strongly and quickly to external stimulus like stress.

Empathic children feel so much and they don't understand how to manage this sensory overload. They experience more emotions. They have more intuition. They smell, hear, and see more. You might realize they don't like certain smells when you are cooking them dinner. A new perfume might make them sick. They may get headaches in harsh lighting or around loud talking. They like soft clothing, nature, beauty, and having just a few close friends.

Their senses get bombarded by the coarseness of the world and this causes changes to their behavior. Most empathic children don't understand why they get upset. Parents that understand them can help find their triggers and give them solutions to help relieve their stress.

As parents, we need to understand what gets our empathic children over stimulated and stay away from these activities. Doing things that keep them calm will help with anxiety, tantrums, and exhaustion.

Most schools and society don't try to understand these exceptional children. Normal teachers and physicians will label them as fussy, antisocial, or shy. They get diagnosed with depression, anxiety disorder, or social phobia. They tend to be gentle, deep, thoughtful, and quieter instead of being assertive and very verbal. Because they have been wrongly diagnosed, your role as a parent is to support their wisdom, creativity, intuition, and sensitivity. We have to teach them a way to cope with their feelings.

The following things can be done to nurture your empathic child:

1. Encourage their imagination

When you are reading or watching a movie with your child, ask them what they think the person might be feeling or thinking. This will encourage their empathy.

2. Acknowledge other's emotions

Your child needs to understand that everybody's emotions are important and they learn everything from you. Make sure that you respect the emotions of others, so they know their emotions are valid.

3. Play pretend

Playing pretend gets a child ready for real life. This also gives them a chance to play around with different emotions when pretending to be different people.

4. Stick with the feeling

When your child is experiencing a strong emotion, help them work through it. Talk with them to figure out what caused the emotion. This will teach them how to handle it.

Children who are empaths are precious beings. It doesn't matter where your child lands on the spectrum, they would benefit from you teaching them about their sensitivities.

Chapter 16: Exercises You Can do Daily

You've made it this far. You should have a pretty good understanding of your gift and you should be proud that you have it. There have been many different exercises explained throughout this book that you can use to hone into your skills and to make your life easier as an empath. I'm going to leave you with a few more exercises that you can do each day if you want.

With the constant bombardment of negative energy in the world, it can be hard for an empath to remain grounded. Staying at home can even prove to be hard if you keep your empathic antennas turned on. Because of all of these issues, it can be easy for you to become drained, distracted from your roles, and consumed by apathy.

To combat all of this, you have to protect yourself in order to remain grounded. Everyone is different, so what works for one may not work for the other. That said, the best way to protect yourself and remain grounded is to build up a resilience, a strong energy field, a healthy body, and a quiet mind.

1. Diet

Another great thing an empath can do is to include nutritious and grounding foods in their diet and get rid of drug-life foods. Wheat is one of the worst offenders. Empaths are sensitive to vibrations. Everything in the world vibrates at different frequencies and this means alcohol, food, and drugs. Things with low vibrations negatively affect empaths. Most alcohol and drugs will have a low vibration and can bring an empath down.

If you are having a hard time staying grounded, even though you are trying to everything, have a look to see what you are eating.

2. Sea Salt

It's believed that Hippocrates, the father of medicine, was one of the first people to figure out sea salt had healing abilities after he noticed how fast seawater could help a fisherman's wounded hand.

Not only can sea salt heal, but it can also purify. It can remove and dissolve bad energies from your physical and emotional body. You will discover that this is great if you have to interact with people, where it is easy to pick up their anxiety and stress.

3. Exercise

While most people exercise to tone their body and lose weight, exercise can do a lot more for an empath. It is a great way to release pent-up emotions, gets rid of impurities through sweat, improves their mood, increases happiness, energizes, creates an energy field, and is grounding.

Do whatever you love to do. If you don't like following rules or routines, crank up some music and dance like nobody's watching.

4. Creativity

Living in a world of routines and rules, most people don't get time to be creative, but this is the easiest way to get into your feel-good time. When you are feeling good, then you are grounded. When you create things from your passions, it uplifts your psyche. When you are engaging in things that you love, it will keep your mind away from dark feelings and thoughts.

5. Nature

Being around nature is very grounding and healing for empaths. As an empath, if you don't spend all that much time in nature, you are going to struggle to feel grounded and remain balanced.

6. Laughter

Grownups tend to spend way too much time being serious and solemn and too little time having real fun. Can you remember the last time you get to enjoy a really good deep belly laugh? Children laugh all the time. They don't take life seriously as we do. They have fun and play, which helps them to remain grounded. It's important that adults strive to be childlike. To see the wonder in the world and have fun and laugh every now and then. Anything that will make you laugh will help boost your spirits.

7. Crystals

Numerous cultures have been using the healing power of crystals. Ancients used to have crystal chambers that they would use to heal energetic, spiritual, and physical ailments. Crystals can be used along with the chakras to help balance them out and get rid of blockages. Since empaths can naturally sense their healing vibrations, they will be drawn to crystals by their instincts for their protective and grounding abilities.

8. Essential oils

Essential oils work just like crystals in their healing powers and have been used just as long. Through the olfactory senses is where the benefits of oils are obtained. You can find oils that help every empath.

9. Earthing

This may be at the bottom of the list, but it is the most beneficial thing that an empath can do to stay grounded. Earthing means that you place your naked feet on the natural earth, so go for a barefoot walk. The healing power of Mother Earth is often taken for granted, yet it is the easiest way to connect and find balance.

There you go. These exercises can be used every single day to help you stay grounded and connected. Find what works best for you and stick with it.

Conclusion

Thank you for making it through to the end of *Empath Emotional Guide*. Let's hope it was informative and able to provide you with all of the tools you need to achieve your goals whatever they may be.

Being an empath is a wonderful gift. It is nothing to be ashamed of even if it is still misunderstood. Empathic skills can help you and those around you if you know how to use them right. Use the different exercises in this book to help you hone in on your skills. The important thing is to make sure that you take care of yourself and heal yourself.

Finally, if you found this book useful in any way, a review on Amazon is always appreciated!

<u>One last thing before you go – Can I ask a small favor?</u> I need your help! If this book has been helpful to you, could you share your experience on Amazon by providing an honest feedback and review? This wouldn't take much of your time (a sentence will be very much appreciated), but a massive help for me and absolutely good Karma. Due to not having the backing of a big publication I don't have the big reach or promotion to get my books out to a bigger audience and rely heavily on my readers help, <u>I take out time to read every review and I'm usually extremely excited for every honest feedback I get. If my book was able to inspire you, please express it!</u> This will help position me at the top for others seeking for new ideas and reasonable knowledge to access easily.

I'm very grateful and I wish you every good things of life on your journey!

Warm regards,
Michael.

My Free Gift to You – <u>Get One of My Audiobooks For Free!</u>

If you've never created an account on Audible (the biggest audiobook store in the world), **<u>you can claim one free</u>** audiobook **<u>of mine!</u>**
It's a simple process:

1. Pick one of audiobooks on Audible: https://www.audible.com/search?keywords=michael+wilkinson&ref=a_search_t1_header_search

2. Once you choose a book and open its detail page click the orange button "Free with 30-Day Trial Membership."

3. Follow the instructions to create your account and download you first free audiobook.

Not that you are NOT obligated to continue after your free trial expires. You can cancel you free trial easily anytime and won't be charged at all.

About The Author

Hello,

My name is Michael. My life has been one amazing and a passionate journey, which I feel want everyone to be a part of or experience in one way or the other. I'm someone who believes there is more to life than what we already know. I endeavored many things to transform my life way more than my expectations to a very fulfilling one, and it's time I shared with you this interesting journey in order for you to apply it, as well.

I was a shy and quiet kid and had the typical young life, growing up in England doing the normal kids things, playing football, video games and didn't know much of what I wanted in life except that I loved cartoons. That was until I turned 18 and started to explore the world. That changed the way I saw things and everything in life, it opened my eyes to what was possible. I became very eager to learn new things and explore more.

My interests include traveling, practicing martial arts, self development, and offering value by assisting other people. I've got a keen passion for contents relating to sociology, mediation, social psychology, eastern philosophy, communication skills, emotional intelligence, NLP, time management, mindfulness, and relevant studies related to self-development and being the best version of whom you are. Calm down, smile, and express the life inside of you... I look forward to hearing from you soon!

Source Material

Acharya, S., & Shukla, S. (2012). Mirror neurons: Enigma of the metaphysical modular brain. *Journal of Natural Science, Biology and Medicine*, 118-124.

Barsade, S. G. (2002). The Ripple Effect: Emotional Contagion and its Influence on Group Behavior. *Administrative Science Quarterly*, 644-675.

Brown, L., Collins, N., Sangster, M.-D., Aron, A., Aron, E., & Acevedo, B. (2014). The highly sensitive brain: a fMRI study of sensory processing sensitivity and response to others' emotions. *Brain and Behavior*, 580-594.

Iacoboni, M. (2009). Imitation, Empathy, and Mirror Neurons. *Annual Reviews of Psychology*, 653-670.

McCraty, R., Atkinson, M., Tomasino, D., & Tiller, W. (1998). The Electricity of Touch: Detection and Measurement of Cardiac Energy Exchange Between People. *Research Library*.

Riess, H. (2017). The Science of Empathy. *Journal of Patient Experience*, 74-77.

www.ingramcontent.com/pod-product-compliance
Lightning Source LLC
Chambersburg PA
CBHW061817250726
48657CB00001B/470